Challenged
to
GROW

Challenged
to
GROW

A Catholic Parent's Journey
Through an Evangelical World

Richard L. Akins

New City Press
Hyde Park, New York

Published by New City Press
202 Comforter Blvd.,
Hyde Park, NY 12538
www.newcitypress.com

Cover design by Leandro De Leon
Book design and layout by Miguel Tejerina

Library of Congress Control Number: 2017956501

ISBN: 978-1-56548-625-6 paperback
ISBN: 978-1-56548-626-3 e-book

Printed in the United States of America

Contents

Chapter 1

Overcoming Christian Disunity

I was in my late thirties, a life-long Catholic, married, and a father of three. Suddenly, to maintain family cohesion I lived part-time within a decidedly anti-Catholic "Evangelical"[1] faith community, attending their services at least every other week.

As a teen, I joined an inter-denominational youth group run by Evangelicals. During my high school years those sessions tapped into and ignited my passion for Christ. Later, as an adult, I listened to Evangelical radio broadcasts while commuting to work for at least two decades. My very best friend, who died all too young, was an Evangelical. I never considered that any of these Evangelicals risked eternal damnation simply because they didn't share my Catholic beliefs.

And—lucky day!—as I scoured the well-worn pages of my Catholic Catechism, I found that the Church agreed. The official teaching of my Catholic faith is that baptized Christians of other denominations are saved by

---

1. I will use the term "Evangelical" because this is the title used most often by those I have attended services with. However, the term "Evangelical" describes people who may hold a wide range of beliefs. To be more precise, then, those I have lived with and experienced as often the most aggressively divisive may also use the additional titles "Reformed," "Calvinistic" and "Bible-Believing." I will also use these terms where appropriate in this work.

Christ. In fact, the Church teaches that God might lead even those who are not Christian to recognize something of the Truth. Regardless of their expressed beliefs, we all share the same creator God and this creator God can be creative enough to call all kinds of people and even save them, if he so chooses.

Only months after we began attending the Evangelical church, my son—then eight years old—changed from not wanting to go to the new church to not wanting to go back to our Catholic parish (in which he had just received his first Communion) because the music in the new church was more exciting. Occasionally, the children in his age group at the new church performed child-oriented skits. My son was entertained. To a child, isn't that all-important? Shouldn't I strive to keep him and my two daughters interested in going to church?

But a large and startled part of me protested, "That is *not* all-important. Not by a long shot."

No, the important issue is to come to Christ. To lead a Christian life, in the way Christ and those who lived with him taught, so we can create a better life here for ourselves, our families, and our world; but more critically to find ourselves one day in a much better and eternal life with Christ.

Isn't that what "religion" and faith is for? Didn't I long ago commit—vow, in fact—that in the raising of my children and in my married life, I would follow and teach faith in Christ as the Catholic Church confesses?

Hitting Close to Home

The relatively small Evangelical church we initially attended part-time soon gave way to a "mega" church. My "Sure, we'll go to Protestant services occasionally" turned into attending this megachurch three or even four times a month. However, as time passed and my youngest daughter missed the entire year of Catholic education leading to her first Communion, I faced a growing daily struggle.

Was I doing the right thing? When I was confirmed, I committed myself to the Church and the Holy Spirit. I promised to bring my children up Catholic. I promised during our wedding, celebrating the sacrament of matrimony, to live out a Catholic life. Now I felt a threat to the unity and future of our family. How could my most intimate relationships survive if we could not share the most intimate matters of faith?

Were my intentions of seeing other Christians as fellow Christ-followers false? Was my view of Christian unity and fellowship a reality, or was it just a nice sentiment to make myself feel better as long as other Christian expressions of the faith remained outside myself and my family?

An Ecumenical Upbringing

Over the past eighteen years, I have gone from listening to, reading, and appreciating Evangelical leaders on the radio, Internet and bookshelves, to scrutinizing what they teach, why they teach what they teach, and the outcomes of those theologies. Facing new challenges raised by my Evangelical brethren, I looked equally hard

at my Catholic faith. I and my children were now questioned by good and sincere Christians who denied we
Catholics were even Christian. In fact, many held that
we are instead enemies of God. How should I address
these issues?

Could I lead my Evangelical brethren to a deeper
appreciation and acceptance of the "Christian" nature of
the Catholic faith? Could I transfer to my fellow Catholics
some of the ideas and practices of the Evangelical churches
I find beneficial for our 2000-year-old expression of the
faith?

I decided long ago that I didn't have all the answers.
Perhaps—just perhaps—my church didn't have all the
answers. To this day the Catholic Church holds councils and synods to address the needs and questions of a
changing world. I never felt I and my fellow Catholics
alone could be saved. The Catholic Church itself teaches
all validly baptized Christians are part of the catholic
("universal") family of God, part of my church. Perhaps
an *exclusive* perspective on salvation would damage my
ability to love non-Catholics and attract non-believers to
the faith.

At the same time, having been brought up in a
positive and devoted Catholic family, I love the Catholic
faith. I was troubled that Evangelicals believe all truth
is found in the Bible yet at the same time disown the
Catholic Church, which from its earliest centuries gathered, verified, transmitted, studied and taught from those
same biblical texts.

I needed justification, at least for my own peace of
mind, for my being Catholic. For my children, I needed

clear reasons for holding with the Catholic faith, and in a larger sense, for explaining why that faith should be acceptable—at the very least—to the non-Catholic Christians we live among. To be open to "fundamentalist" Evangelical teachings, I also had to expose my children to, and reconcile them with, the "fundamental" Christian faith—Catholicism. Where appropriate, I needed to demonstrate why the Catholic faith is vital for my growth as a Christian and theirs.

In a unique way I have been challenged to grow. I have been led upon a thirteen-year path toward reconciliation. Reconciliation with what God requires, what my personal vows demand, what the future holds for my children and my direction within my church(es). This path is the theme of this book. In short, the theme of discovering the "fundamental" future of my eternal soul.

A Practical Hope

As a Catholic interfacing with a second Christian faith community, I had little appreciation for the questions and challenges I would experience. I quickly realized my Evangelical brethren likewise could not comprehend the questions a Catholic like myself would ask. As I uncovered these challenges and the responses to them, I realized followers of all denominations need to appreciate the various expressions of our Christian faith. Not by choice but through a decade's worth of sometimes difficult life-experiences, I find myself in a unique position to present the truths of Catholicism to those who hold aggressively anti-Catholic beliefs. With due respect for both perspectives, perhaps we can take the first small steps toward unity within our Lord's family.

This is a vital task. As Jesus prays in John 17:20-21, it is by the outward unity of Christians that the world will come to believe that the Father has indeed sent his Son.

The following thoughts gelled as the primary aims of this book:

For Catholics:

- We belong to the "fundamental" Christian faith that Christ brought to the world.
- Our faith is deeply biblical.
- Our faith is additionally effective because it is sacramental.
- Ecumenical outreach to our Christian brothers and sisters is not optional.

For Other Christians:

- The main tenets of our faith are catholic (universal).
- The Bible we read is catholic. There is no single "exclusive" interpretation of scripture.
- The original Reformers did not seek to deny the sacraments of the Church.
- Christ calls on us to also reach out to our Catholic brothers and sisters

Chapter 2

We Can Trust One Another

Fundamentalism

For some, Christian *fundamentalism* suggests outdated, naïve, or old-fashioned beliefs no longer true. Others equate "fundamental" with being "radical." Some claim contemporary Christian radicalism is the same as the radicalism of terrorist sects or others who deny the ideals of freedom. In truth, however, the willingness to lay down one's self, even to the point of death, for the *right cause and in the right way* is the most honorable act of all. Jesus made that clear. If we are in a true relationship with God, then the only appropriate response is to enter that relationship radically, all the while adhering to Christ's call for mercy, love and fellowship.

For many devoted Christians, however, "fundamental" reflects the close connection they believe their faith shares with the truths enunciated by Jesus and the apostles. Unadorned. Unencumbered by time or culture. The true reflection of what Christ himself taught.

From this perspective, Fundamentalism is considered a badge of honor. For many, Fundamentalism in Christianity points back to the fundamental book of the faith—the Bible. Fundamentalists try to determine the meaning of words from the context of what they

13

read and feel closer to the truth by remaining faithful to what they perceive to be the original intent of what was written. In some ways, this is similar to contemporary American political conservatives who find bedrock truth and meaning in the original, fundamental documents from the nation's founding.

But, there is a critical difference.

The fundamental underpinning of America might be the Constitution and Bill of Rights written and agreed to by its founding fathers, but Christianity does not rest upon human documents or human decisions. Ultimately, Christianity is not based upon a text. The faith is not based, ultimately, upon the Bible.

Christianity is based upon a *person*—the God-man, Jesus Christ. Before there was a complete and recognized New Testament, generations of men and women followed Christ, tens of thousands converted to the faith, and the Church grew at an astounding rate even under the direst of persecutions. We have sacred scripture, to be sure, but even more we have the historical figure of Christ, the miracle worker, the teacher and sage, the Messiah, the *risen* Lord, God the Son, showing us the path to salvation.

Jesus, in his perfect God-wisdom, knew how to lead a people toward salvation. He defined salvation. Throughout the world and throughout time people have been saved by him, the Second Person of the Trinity, without Jesus writing (directly) a single word. In his wisdom, he built the foundation of his place in-and-above history not upon a book, but through a group of people. His apostles. His Church.

"Fundamental" Christianity, then, is reflected truly and positively not by those who follow one interpretation of the Bible as we know it today, but those who most closely follow the fundamental Church Jesus established. Still, as this Church grew and spread the inspired accounts concerning its founder's life convey Christianity's core beliefs and doctrines. In the 300s and early 400s the Church discerned the Bible as we now know it. While that Bible did not document everything the Church understood about Christ—no single book ever could—it contained eye-witness accounts of Jesus and doctrines that church leaders of the day found consistent with the faith as it had long been practiced. Core Christian beliefs (in the Trinity, etc.) that all Christians still share also came from those early centuries of the Church. We can and should build upon this shared foundation so that, even as we debate some theological issues, we can see (and show the world) we are all believers in Christ and brothers and sisters to one another.

These insights allowed me to consider both of my faith families—my newly adopted Evangelical family and the Catholic family of my upbringing—in a positive light. I did not see that one denomination and interpretation needed to win over the other; I saw two faiths that share many core beliefs. Each seeks in good faith to live faithfully according to what Christ wanted.

Words have power. Just as the army that gains the high ground traditionally wins the battle, so too the first meaning attached to a word shapes the character of a debate. "Fundamentalist" or "Bible-believing" churches see themselves as following the fundamentals of the faith Christ brought. Historically, however, they have sprung from other, more fundamental Protestant faiths, which in turn derived from a yet more fundamental Catholic religion. The "fundamentalist" tag has stuck, however, and for many Evangelicals the term represents a belief that their form of the faith reflects more closely the fundamental teachings of the Christian founder. By further implication, churches not considered "fundamental" are less true to the origins of Christianity and have added to their religious expression things that are not in line with what Christ intended.

The practices of a church (language, time and frequency of prayers, etc.) can obviously be changed without changing the key teachings handed down by Jesus through the apostles. Jesus gave those apostles authority and promised guidance of the Holy Spirit to "the end of the age." This implies that our faith is alive, capable of changing to meet the needs of multiple cultures, political realities, and technological advances, as it has for over two thousand years. The Holy Spirit's guidance has no expiration date. New challenges and circumstances require new answers, building upon the faith passed down to us.

To make a practical analogy ... As a father, we may explain to our children the 'fundamental' nature of our faith in terms of a chocolate chip cookie. Every chocolate chip cookie has a fundamental recipe that includes certain ingredients; sugar and flour, sugars and vanilla, eggs and chocolate chips, and a pinch of salt. Many Evangelicals consider only one "ingredient" to be vital: a particular interpretation of the written Bible. Reducing the number of ingredients that make up a thing, however, does not make that thing turn out better. A cookie made of only flour and eggs may be simpler, but it is no longer—fundamentally—a chocolate chip cookie. To create the treat everyone expects, a chef needs to employ all seven ingredients.

On the other hand, fundamentalists do have a point. We should not just keep adding things to our recipe. Adding macadamia nuts, for example, might enhance the taste of the cookie. But adding onions or pickle juice would ruin our treat. So, we must not strip too much away, nor should we add things (in terms of theology and practice) without very careful consideration. Either approach might not produce what God had in mind.

A Pop Culture View of the Divide

I have experienced only one branch of Evangelical Protestantism, the form referred to as "Reformed" and theologically Calvinistic—that is, generally following the principles of Protestant leader John Calvin (1509-1564). This form of Christianity is aggressively and vocally anti-Catholic (and often anti- "mainline" Protestant as well). Since it is almost impossible to entertain thoughts of ecumenism and Christian unity if one denomination does not consider the other as Christian at all, dialogue is vital to fulfilling Jesus' prayer at the Last Supper.

Calvinistic Evangelicals believe that some people have been individually chosen as the "elect," whereas all others are predestined through God's sovereign plan to lack (or be denied) saving faith in Christ. As I began my journey, I faced challenges from those who considered

my faith and the faith of my children and all whom I
hold dear to be false. I was told I held a mistaken view
of the Christian faith, and that being Catholic made me
unacceptable to Jesus to the point of being his enemy.

This perspective became clear when our megachurch pastor invited a woman from the congregation
to give her "testimony." She shared the story of her
father, who once had studied to become a priest and who
remained Catholic even after she became Evangelical.
For a decade and more, she prayed for his "conversion" to
"Christianity." She was desperate for him to be "saved,"
to reach a state she obviously did not believe was possible for Catholics. She told us—in front of my Catholic
children—how her father, as a Catholic, believed he was
saved only "through works" and not through faith in the
Lord. Then, lying on his deathbed, he finally pronounced
(to the clapping "alleluia" relief of our megachurch brethren) the correct words and "came to Christ."

After thirteen years of living between two versions
of Christianity, I have come to recognize this as one of the
greatest challenges Christians face. The "fundamental"
one, if you will; the divide that began with the rise of the
Protestant movement and now, five hundred years later,
continues to split our church. Both Evangelical churches
we attended maintained a stereotype that Catholics
believe they are saved through "works," through human
efforts alone by following rules prescribed by the Church,
instead of relying upon faith in Jesus.

Conversely, like many Catholics, I came into the
new Evangelical church stereotyping Protestants and
Evangelicals as believing their subsequent actions do not

matter once they confessed faith in Christ as their personal savior. Many refer to this as "once saved, always saved" theology (although personal experience has demonstrated that many Protestants disagree with this view of salvation).

To overcome my prejudices and explain to my children how such stereotypes came to be, I came first to realize our current divisions came about because groups of Christians responded differently in their sincere desire to follow God's call. Some individuals on both sides of the debate may have less than ideal motivations, but until we stop ridiculing or defaming entire groups of people and start discussing the churches' actual doctrines and practices, we will make no progress.

As a Catholic I can justify the actions of the Church over the past five centuries and decry Protestant "reforms" as rupturing the unity for which Jesus himself prayed. But I cannot and should not see the Reformers as wholly mistaken or those who remained faithful to Rome as entirely correct. Good people on both sides of the Reformation acted out of their belief—in the main— that they were doing God's will.

Obviously, someone born into Protestantism will have different prejudices than I do. But even when I as a Catholic look back through history, I understand the multi-national, powerful Catholic Church of the Middle Ages strayed in various practical ways from Christ's mandate. It had set up many wonderful activities to maintain the faith of believers, to help meet the twin commandments of loving God and loving one's neighbors. But instead of promoting these actions as natural actions performed by lovers of Christ, the stigma of sin was often applied to those who did not participate in those activities. In other words, the mantra sometimes turned from "Do these things because you love Christ and his body, the Church" into, "Do these things we command because if you don't obey it is a sin and you will be punished." The "work" itself drifted toward greater importance than the purpose or goal behind the effort.

Catholic clergy held the keys to forgiveness, salvation, and damnation. Since the all-too-human clerics could not see within a person's heart to determine their faith in and love for God, forgiveness or conviction came to be based more and more upon the externally visible works of the believer. These works, rightly, sometimes involved financial gifts and sacrifices to help God's work on earth, just as religious leaders still ask the faithful for donations. Some Catholics, like Martin Luther, believed that money became the primary object of concern, the gauge by which the Christian was considered justified or cast aside by God. Some believed this led the faithful to the idea that "buying" forgiveness and salvation took the place of recognizing Jesus as our Savior.

Is this true? Well, at the Council of Trent, decades after the Reformation began, the Catholic Church concurred with some of Luther's charges and instituted change.

Although this is a highly simplified overview of the issues underlying the Reformation, Luther's protest indeed did focus upon his opposition to selling "indulgences," gifting money to the church in exchange for remission of sin.

Luther argued that faithful Christians could not earn their way into heaven. No human action or financial gift could merit God "owing" us our eternal reward. However, this idea caused Luther and his followers a problem. If salvation is not connected to external works, then what is it based upon? If the traditional works of mercy, like giving money to the poor, no longer indicated a believer's relationship with God, what *could* give Christians spiritual and mental comfort?

Protestants came to consider the sole gauge for salvation to be "faith." Anything else would lead to the same problem the Reformers sought to overcome, burdening the faithful with tasks unnecessary to their salvation. The "faith" that assures salvation, however, had to be more than a personal feeling. In other words, believers could not claim to be saved merely by feeling positive about God and clinging to Jesus as their Savior. Many factors affect *feelings* concerning faith—health and attitudes, for example, or a simple lack of sleep or poor family and work relationships. Salvation could not sway in and out of existence depending upon the person's moment-to-moment feelings about God.

No, justification had to be—*had* to be—achieved once and for all by claiming faith in Christ. Salvation had to be *assured* from that point forward. Nothing else would do.

Prior to the Reformation, Christian believers knew they would be directed toward heaven by professing faith in Christ, being baptized, living as a member of the Church, receiving the Eucharist, performing good works and charity, and seeking forgiveness through the sacrament of reconciliation. Now, without the Church and the guideposts of observable works and charity, without the Eucharist and the sacrament of reconciliation (both of which were perceived by some as a clerical tool of control), there remained only reliance on faith alone. What if, during the various seasons of life, moods, and circumstances, a believer's faith itself was tested and even perhaps even denied? Would that believer then be damned?

No. The Reformers *needed* to maintain that salvation through faith was permanent, "once for all." And why would some be saved "once for all" and others not? Because those who claimed faith in Jesus did so God had chosen for them individually to possess the true faith all others lacked.

The Evangelicals I know hold with a form of being "saved once for all," but for a slightly different reason. They have been taught that if they weren't saved once for all—if, for example, they could claim faith at one point and then lose salvation later by committing a grievous sin or denying Jesus later in life—it would deny God's sovereign power. The power to say to one person "you will be saved," and to another "you will not." The choice has to be God's, not ours. God is sovereign; we have no power to deny him.

But if salvation does not depend upon a one-time profession of faith, this does not suggest a God who changes his mind about us or lacks the power to have us live out his desire. On the contrary, the Father is sovereign because the universe follows his plan, a plan that we exercise our human wills and, as loving children, come back voluntarily to him through love of Christ. This *sovereign* plan doesn't change despite what we believe or don't believe, nor is it affected by what we do. If we choose to believe and obey, God will follow through with his plan and we will be saved. The Father will not later decide that faith in Jesus is no longer his plan for salvation. If we deny Christ, he again will not accommodate his plan to our state of mind. God will, however, provide the opportunity—should we choose it—to change our minds.

Regardless, the first Reformers and most of those who adhere to their understanding of the relationship between God and human beings hold tight to the concept of salvation through faith alone, once-for-all. Having renounced the authority of tradition, they base their belief upon the only other point of theological authority—the Bible. Thus arose their reliance upon a particular approach to scripture—*sola scriptura*, or "scripture alone."

The general theological concepts of the Reformation are summarized in the *solas* ("sola" meaning "only" or "alone"). Five have been articulated, but the three key solas are *sola fide* ("faith alone" in Jesus), *sola scriptura* ("scripture alone" as ultimate authority in Christian faith), and *sola gratia* ("grace alone," not human merit). Sola scriptura proposes that authority does not reside in the Holy Spirit working through the Church. The new Reformed churches could read the Bible independently and determine how to apply their interpretation of the written word. Sola fide (and its close cousin sola gratia) meant the faithful need not concern themselves about sacraments or feast days or other rituals since salvation came not through their own activities, but only through faith in Christ, given graciously only to those God chose.

These are a few of the historical beliefs that fostered and fueled the Reformation. In our day to day life, the *possibility* of such a divide—one side being right on this issue (and blessed with salvation) and the other wrong (and doomed to damnation)—separates one expression of Christian faith from another.

For example, the Catholic Church considers all those baptized into the Trinity to be brothers and sisters in Christ, and I've met many Evangelicals who treat Catholics with similar respect. But others consider discussions regarding Christian unity as false and harmful. They conclude those who do not hold their beliefs in sola fide and sola scriptura are already damned, that those who believe in Christ but do not express their faith in the same way they do are not truly Christian and God has predestined them for hell.

In *Mere Christianity*, C.S. Lewis maintains that if we see each other as predestined for salvation, we can see each other as eternal, immortal, glorified brothers and sisters. But if we don't, we will think of each other as damned—as eternal, immortal inhabitants of hell. With that outlook, trying to patch of the hundreds of smaller differences between Christian faiths would mean nothing. To do so would mean compromising ourselves with eternal and mortal enemies.

During my fifty years of attending Mass, I have never heard any Roman Catholic priest mention that Christians who hold different beliefs concerning the details of the faith and scripture are permanently lost and enemies of God. Although the Evangelicals I have met hold varying opinions and emphasis, they certainly have a more exclusive and negative view of those who do not conform with their beliefs. This was summarized by R.C. Sproul, who until his death in 2017 had been a leading Reformed Evangelical theologian: "But we must not assume that we are brothers and sisters with them in the gospel. They [Catholics] are members of a church that has anathematized the gospel, so we ought to pray for them and seek to reach them for Christ." [2]

For true reconciliation and unity, Christians need to consider that our stereotypes may not be factual. And we need to pray for those whose beliefs differ from ours; for no one lies beyond God's salvation.

Let's take a closer look at our stereotypes by going to the movies.

The Godfather—Salvation through Works?

The primary Evangelical argument with Catholicism is starkly portrayed at the end of the first *Godfather* movie. Al Pacino, the new Godfather, stands proudly with his infant nephew at the baptismal font of a Catholic church his family supports financially. In his well-dressed propriety, speaking for the child entering the Christian faith, he accepts the faith and rejects the works of Satan.

Meanwhile … well … meanwhile we see snippets of his henchmen going about town murdering his family's enemies.

This sequence illustrates the stereotypical Catholic who performs "works" designated by the Church—but works clearly not leading toward salvation.

---

2. https://www.ligonier.org/blog/how-should-protestants-relate-roman-catholics/

The Apostle—Saved Once for All?

A decade or two later the less-viewed but fine movie, *The Apostle* Robert Duvall, portrays a fire-and-brimstone Bible-thumping Evangelical pastor.

Saved by faith alone. Follower of the Bible alone. Saved, once-for-all.

A "fundamentalist."

And yet … and yet … he murders.

Though not entirely his fault, he nonetheless kills a man. Although he should consider himself "saved" by faith in Jesus alone and through his fundamental Evangelical beliefs "once-for-all"—even from this horrendous sin—he still runs away in shame.

A Catholic watching this part of the movie may think, "How can this person still believe he is saved? Does he believe that just because he once said the magic words 'Christ is Lord' he can do whatever he wants, even murder, as if his actions don't matter at all?"

These films represent what some Protestants challenge about Catholicism, and the theological inconsistency Catholics find in the Reformed Church. But in these two films a patient and discerning movie-goer can also find a possible step toward Christian unity.

In the *Godfather, Part III*, many years and countless sins have taken their toll on Al Pacino's character. In Rome—at the Vatican itself—the Godfather speaks to a church prelate. The monsignor bemoans that in Europe men grow up surrounded by Christianity, yet many do not let Christ penetrate their souls.

The Godfather is clearly torn by what he has done in his life.

The clergyman offers him the sacrament of reconciliation. The Don says "Your eminence ... I am beyond redemption. What is the point of confessing if I don't repent."

Michael Corleone believes his sins cannot be forgiven, and something within us agrees, for the guilt of his murders and other treacheries is great. But the priest insists that surely the blood of Christ can forgive even this murderer's transgressions. Reluctantly, the Godfather begins to bare his soul. Clearly, he realizes that attending weekly Mass, providing financial gifts to the church, and reciting the "Our Father" a thousand times over has not and cannot lead to his salvation.

And neither does the Catholic Church. The shocked and saddened monsignor says, "You can be redeemed, but I know ... you will not change." In their hearts both men believe only a healed relationship with Christ can save. The priest completes the sacrament, absolving the Godfather of his sins in "the name of the Father, and the Son, and Holy Spirit," and commends the Godfather's eternal soul to the mercy of God, just as the Church does for all believers at each Mass.

And as for Robert Duvall?

Well, his character isn't so sure after all that he has been saved through faith alone, once-for-all. Fleeing from justice, he eventually stands at the edge of a pond in another small southeastern town. He cries out for forgiveness, admits his sins, and then immerses himself once, twice, and a third time into the water, in "the name of the Father, and of the Son, and of the Holy Spirit."

By "re-baptizing" himself he comes again into proper relationship with God. Evangelicals sigh with relief that this man of God has come back to the Lord. And in his actions, Catholics see him being reconciled, a practice of the Church for the past two thousand years— a sinner restored to a state of grace after confessing their sins. We are not saved once-for-all but need to return repeatedly to repent before the Lord.

These artistic works present Catholic and Protestant stereotypes, but they also deconstruct them. At heart, *The Godfather* and *The Apostle* in key ways are the same. Looking at both of my Christian families with the eyes of the other and considering their arguments, I have come to understand we all believe roughly the same concerning these critical theological issues-redemption, reconciliation, and salvation.

Evangelicals in good faith and Catholics in good faith are both Christian, both redeemed, even if we don't see each other that way. We can both live within our own "truth" and not condemn the other side. We certainly should no longer testify that those who do not believe exactly as we do are not Christian.

Faith Discussion with Kids

The "testimony" of the Evangelical woman who considered her Catholic father lost until his deathbed conversion prompted me to write the following letter to my children. In the heat of that moment, I explain the connection between faith and works, to show how Catholic doctrine is fully Christian and scriptural. Perhaps this can offer practical support for any Christian parent trying to wade through the noise our children face every day.

My Children—

Not all Christian churches maintain a healthy relationship and outlook toward one another. That type of attitude is destructive. For it is one matter to believe our own expression of the Christian faith is what God wants in terms of worship, or that our beliefs more closely follow what Jesus taught, or that our own church can best convey the faith to the next generation and spread the gospel throughout the world. It is another matter altogether to promote one form of Christianity by destroying others, telling those faithful people they are not truly Christian, that they are lost souls.

Since Jesus Christ came to earth two thousand years ago, there has been a Christian Church, a "universal" Christian Church, the "catholic" Christian Church. Today's Catholics see that non-Catholic Christians hold with many parts of this same faith. At various times and for various reasons, groups have broken from full membership ("communion") with the Church. While some accept concepts not considered Christian, most churches still maintain the core principles of the faith.

- There is a God who created everything and who is interested and active in our lives.

- God gave us human will, and because of this we are able to commit sins against each other and against God.

- Jesus Christ, who is God, came to earth to live among us and die for our sins. If we believe this and repent of our sins, we will be forgiven and will live for eternity with God in heaven.

As churches split off from one another, some people condemned those who did not leave as non-Christian, unworthy of Christ's forgiveness. Some accuse the Catholic Church of teaching we do not have to have a relationship with Jesus, that we only need to be "good enough" to "earn" our way into heaven. On the other hand, some Catholics believe that others, having professed faith in Christ, think they can sin all they want the rest of their lives. Both are false stereotypes. Our actual beliefs regarding salvation are not that far apart.

The Catholic Church teaches we are forgiven through faith in Jesus. But the Church also maintains the biblical concept that faith without works is "dead." To be truly in union with Christ, we need to be changed people, doing good and avoiding evil. The argument that Catholics don't believe in salvation through faith in Christ is refuted by many passages from the *Catechism of the Catholic Church*, and from the Bible:

- "Believing in Jesus Christ and the God who sent him is necessary for obtaining salvation, without faith no one has attained justification."[3]

---

3. *Catechism of the Catholic Church, Second Edition* (New York: Doubleday, 1995), paragraph 161.

- But, as St. Paul said to Timothy, we can lose this gift: "I am giving you these instructions, Timothy, my child, in accordance with the prophecies made earlier about you, so that by following them you may fight the good fight, having faith and a good conscience. By rejecting conscience, certain persons have suffered shipwreck in the faith." (1 Timothy 1:18-19)

To persevere in saving faith in Christ we must "nourish it with the word of God; we must beg the Lord to increase our faith; it must be "working through charity," abounding in hope, and rooted in the faith of the Church" (*Catechism*, 162).

The *Catechism* continues,

- "Faith is the beginning to eternal life" (163).

- "Salvation comes from God alone" (169).

- Citing Thomas Aquinas, the *Catechism* states "We do not believe in formulas [e.g. prayers and creeds] but in those realities they express, which faith allows us to touch. The believer's act [of faith] does not terminate in the propositions, but in the realities [which they express]" (170).

- "But 'faith apart from works is dead': when it is deprived of hope and love, faith does not fully unite the believer to Christ and does not make him a living member of his Body." (*Catechism* 1815)

- "The grace of the Holy Spirit has the power to justify us, that is, to cleanse us from our sins and to communicate to us 'the righteousness of

God through faith in Jesus Christ' and through Baptism." (*Catechism* 1987)

- "But if we have died with Christ, we believe that we will also live with him. We know that Christ, being raised from the dead, will never die again; death no longer has dominion over him. The death he died, he died to sin, once for all; but the life he lives, he lives to God. So you also must consider yourselves dead to sin and alive to God in Christ Jesus." (Romans 6: 6-11)

It is a biblical truth that we need to act out our faith, that our faith produces good works and not just good feelings within ourselves. Such ideas align with numerous statements in the Gospels where Jesus states clearly those who would follow him need to believe in him and have faith that he has come to save us from our sins. But also, that we must show our love for him through our obedience to his commands.

He had scathing words for religious hypocrites, whose hearts were evil but made great public show of their faith, as if their outward trivialities meant anything to God. He is clear that faith in him will bring us to life, as in John 5:24, "Very truly, I tell you, anyone who hears my word and believes him who sent me has eternal life, and does not come under judgement, but has passed from death to life."

But his words also emphasize the fruits of our works that come about because we believe in him not only as Savior but as Lord. For example:

- In Matthew 25: 31-46, Jesus says many will claim that they know him, but he will reject them from heaven, telling them that they did not *feed* him when they saw him hungry, or *clothe* him when they found him naked.

- To the rich young man who wished to know how to achieve eternal life, Jesus first says to follow the commandments, and *do* (honor your mother and father) or not *do* (adultery, murder, etc.) what they command. Only then does he say that the young man should believe in him, sell all his possessions (again, "doing"), and follow. (Mt 19: 16-21)

And, in the verses directly following John 5:24, Jesus says: "The hour is coming when all who are in their graves will hear his voice and will come out—those who have done good, to the resurrection of life, and those who have done evil, to the resurrection of condemnation of the dead" (Jn 5:28-29).

Of course, every believer in Christ should do good works in gratitude for the salvation we have received through his sacrifice. But we should also do good works, following Jesus' own example, to build and maintain our faith in him. Jesus' actions and words emphasize equally our need for faith in him, *and* our need to respond to this faith by living a changed life for each other. All true Christian teaching needs to reflect this dual reality.

Love, Dad

The Gospel

In 325, church leaders came together at Nicaea to address various heresies. In doing so, they clarified faith and doctrine. These beliefs are expressed in the Nicene Creed (similar tenets are also expressed in the Apostles' Creed). For almost 1200 years—up until the Reformation—the Nicene Creed defined authentic Christian belief. Today, some claim this creed no longer defines what the members of Christ's *true* church believe. They maintain that to truly follow Christ, it is necessary to believe in the Trinity, but you have to believe in a specific "gospel."

As the examples from *The Godfather* and *The Apostle* demonstrate, Catholics and many Protestants hold nearly identical beliefs concerning justification. But Christians are still badly divided, so the question remains: what are these differing definitions of "gospel"? And do these differences justify the divisions within our family?

At a national conference, a leading American Evangelical figure defined the "Good News" simply as having faith in Jesus as our savior, whereby our sins are imputed (transferred) to Christ, and the righteousness of Christ is simultaneously imputed to us, a process known as "cross-imputation." The justification provided by faith in Christ through the imputation of our sins upon him forgives us of all our sins—past, present, and future.

Following the fall of Adam, the souls of every human being were thought to have degenerated into a state of depravity that prevents accepting God and his ways. The Good News, then, is that God chose to "regenerate" certain individuals who now can accept Christ as their savior. Once Christ is accepted, the debt of all their sins is cancelled. This Evangelical interpretation of the gospel leads toward the concept of "once saved-always saved"; if a believer's future sins are already forgiven, how can that person not continue to be saved? It also leads to a belief that among all those who claim faith in Christ, only one group truly understands and believes in this "double" imputation. They are the elect; everyone else is lost.

In practice, most people (like Robert Duvall's apostle) do not believe in a once-saved, always-saved reality. If Christ takes upon himself *all* our sins, then should we not take on *all* his righteousness? While on earth, Christ's righteousness was not hidden, visible only to the Father. In fact, one of the proofs the apostles used to support the claim of Jesus' divinity was his sinless nature and life while on Earth.

Also, if our faith comes only from God's eternal choice, then why would the Evangelical "witness" mentioned in chapter 2 pray for her father's conversion and insist that he make a deathbed decision to come to Jesus? That would not be her father's choice, but one already made by the Father. And yet, she instinctively knew the truth. Her father had the choice to respond and to repent and had to claim faith. Her prayers to the Father for her father in this regard mattered.

As I entered deeper into Evangelicalism, this idea of "cross-imputation" made me uncomfortable. If this is the Good News, it would seem God pretends we are something we are not. Our souls, however soiled, are considered clean simply because Jesus' soul is clean. Saying the Father no longer sees our sins because our guilt is passed on to Christ and Christ's righteousness is passed on to us, is essentially saying the same thing in two ways. We are claiming God no longer sees our guilt because he sees only Jesus' righteousness and so imputes the blame for our sins not on us, but on Christ.

I do not present this view of "cross-imputation" to refute it, but to explain it. If our fellow Christians are truly our brothers or sisters in Christ, we must understand what they believe and do, and why they do so. If we understand the doctrines they believe, we will not consider challenges to our own faith to be unfounded attacks by enemies. We can patiently listen and answer, understanding that those who challenge us are acting out of sincere love for Christ.

Evangelicals believe that in the true believer two things take place. First, the Father does place our sins, as it were, into Christ's account and no longer punishes us for these failings. At the same time, our natural fallen state that made us incapable of wanting or following God is replaced with a new nature, the righteous nature of Jesus. We can then desire to become true sons and daughters of God because our new natures allow it.

But believers who claim faith in Christ as savior don't automatically receive Christ's righteousness. The case can be made, as did C.S. Lewis in *Mere Christianity*, that justification does not make instant saints of all who convert to Christianity, but "If Christianity is true then it ought to follow that any Christian will be nicer than the same person would be if he were not a Christian."[4] In other words, accepting Christ puts us on the path of growing in his righteousness. Our sins being imputed immediately and completely upon Christ does not confer immediate and complete righteousness as proof of our faith. It does mean that our coming to Christ allows us to begin our process toward righteous sanctification.

In Catholic terms, faith in Christ gives us an initial level of sanctifying grace. Our original sin is forgiven, and personal sins to that point in our lives. The ongoing work of sanctification, the ongoing transfer, if you will, of Christ's righteousness to us, is explained in terms of receiving actual graces by which we, cooperating with God's ongoing call, receive support as we grow in the righteousness of Christ, and forgiveness of our ongoing sins should we repent.

If Evangelicals believe salvation consists in Christ taking on our guilt and giving us his righteousness, a similarly succinct statement of Catholic doctrine concerning the gospel would be useful.

The Catholic view might be stated this way: Christ's sacrifice is payment enough for the sins of all who in faith claim him as their Savior. However, in all aspects of the incarnate Christ's interaction with the world (his being, his teachings, his example, the Spirit he sent after the Ascension, and the Church he commanded built prior to his Ascension), he is also our Lord and helps those

---

4. *Mere Christianity* (New York: Harper One, 1952), 210.

who choose to cooperate in obedience with the will of the Father. We must have faith in Christ as Savior, and we must obey Jesus as Lord.

Are Catholic and Evangelical understandings of the gospel close enough that we can accept each other as fellow Christ followers? Perhaps it would be helpful to look again at the term, "gospel," which means "Good News."

What is the good about the news of Christianity? The good is that God, through our faith and dependence upon Christ, forgives our sins. But to Catholics, it is not only "good" that God gives us some share in Christ's righteousness, it is also "good" that we then receive help and guidance to obey God's commands. In other words, Christ tells us that if we are "pruned" we will produce real fruits (Jn 15:1-2); Paul urges us to work hard to maintain our faith to the end; the Holy Spirit is sent to give us wisdom so we can understand God's desires for us and to provide the graces that help us obey. These are key components of the "good news" of the Christian "gospel."

The Good News, then, concerns not only what happens to us in the next life; it includes our sanctification—our becoming like Christ—here and now. For it is our Christ-likeness in this world that leads to a proper relationship with each other and to building up of the family of Christ.

Living in the Evangelical world, I had to discern when my view of the gospel led to division. There are three main ways our view of the gospel can impede our acceptance of those who believe differently. First, the definition of "gospel" can affect our interpretation of the Bible. Next, it can have practical consequences when dealing with the basic theology, or tradition, of the Church. Finally, differences can lead to a disunity that affects our brotherhood in Christ, our ability to worship together, receive the sacraments, and evangelize the world for Christ.

For example, believing God alone chooses whether individuals are to have permanent faith in Christ devalues the practices we use to maintain our faith through difficult times. Following the Church's spiritual practices does not *earn* a person salvation *without* Jesus. Such practices serve to maintain a close relationship with God, increase faith in Jesus as savior, and strengthen the ability to serve him as Lord.

If, for example, Catholics see other Christians' allegiance to scripture alone as a denial of the Holy Spirit's authority to engage the new challenges of a changing world, they must understand that this stance is not held due to pride and obstinacy but from a sincere determination to keep the faith purely passed down through the ages, placing trust in God's words in the scriptures and not in what that believer considers a changeable human institution. The "rightness" of a Catholic or an Evangelical view of the gospel, therefore, can be argued. But, no one should see the others' view in terms of good or evil.

On to the "Minors"?

One critical issue separating Catholic and Evangelical Christians is the different emphasis upon faith and works;

another is the different understanding of human will[5]
versus predestination. Catholics (and some Protestants)
believe in a personal, involved, merciful, and loving
Father. A Father who offers salvation to all who choose
to believe through faith in Jesus but who also has created
human beings with the freedom to follow or to reject
this path. Other Protestants (specifically those who call
themselves "Evangelical" and "Calvinist") stress the all-
powerful nature and sovereignty of an omnipotent Father
who predestined the "born again," or "elect," to receive
individually and exclusively what they need for salvation.

Both sides cite the Bible and early church fathers
to support their positions. When I began to attend an
Evangelical church, however, I realized neither they nor
Catholics tend to articulate their theological underpin-
nings to those "in the pews." Lack of understanding generates distrust and conflict, perpetuating the idea we have
irreconcilable differences and forestalling mutual respect
within our common Christian family.

Catholics like myself (who generally hold with the
"free-will" position) find it difficult to believe God predestines some for salvation, because the logical conclusion
is that others must then be predestined for damnation.

---

5. You may have noticed I have used the term "human will" a few times already
in this book, not "free will." Later, the term "free will" appears in other official
documents I cite. In conversation with Evangelicals it is apparent that "free will"
is considered just that—*entirely* free. But no Christian believes we have *entirely* free
wills. If God, who alone truly has free will, decides to do something in our lives,
that thing will be done. He is God. But, God did grant every human being a will,
a "human will." We are not puppets, nor are we robots. God gave us human will
so we can turn our will back toward him in true and worthwhile love.

The *Catechism of the Catholic Church* states:

God predestines no one to go to hell; for this,
a willful turning away from God (a mortal
sin) is necessary, and persistence in it until
the end. In the Eucharistic liturgy and in
the daily prayers of her faithful, the Church
implores the mercy of God, who does not
want any to perish, but all to come to repentance. (1037)

This interpretation comes directly from biblical sources, such as 2 Peter 3:9: "The Lord
… is patient with you, not wanting any to
perish, but all to come to repentance."

Those who believe in the strict concept of the
"elect"—those predestined from the beginning of time to
receive saving faith from God—tend to cite two passages
from the Letter to the Ephesians:

… [J]ust as he chose us in Christ before
the foundation of the world to be holy and
blameless before him in love. He destined us
for adoption as his children through Jesus
Christ, according to the good pleasure of his
will, to the praise of his glorious grace that he
freely bestowed on us in the Beloved. (Eph
1:4-6)

In Christ we have also obtained an inheritance, having been destined according to the

purpose of him who accomplishes all things
according to his counsel and will, so that we,
who were the first to set our hope on Christ,
might live for the praise of his glory. (Eph
1:11-12)

Evangelicals who hold with predestination cite
these texts to conclude that God sees all human beings
as naturally evil and doomed to just punishment. But,
according to the plan formed from the creation of the
world, God chose to be merciful to a small group of the
elect. He is not indebted to this group, does not *owe*
them a reward for good behavior, but saves them simply
so he can be glorified for his mercy.

As a Catholic, the passages from Ephesians indicate
to me that those who claim and maintain Christian faith
should be thankful to the Father, whose eternal plan is
for Christ to provide us a path to salvation. Strengthened
by the Holy Spirit, we use our God-given human will to
accept and maintain our faith. By remaining obedient to
God, we belong to a family of believers predestined for
salvation. The passages from Ephesians do not mean that
from the beginning of time some individuals, instead
of and above all others, were individually chosen to be
saved.

Perhaps what Paul meant in Ephesians (in addition to promoting personal humility before the Lord)
was that for all eternity the Father planned to send Jesus
to bring the Christian faith and establish the Christian
Church. From this respect, we—as a communal church
and whole people of God—have been eternally chosen to

exist and to provide a path for the world's salvation. But individually we still struggle like everyone else to make it and sometimes fail. To stay within Christ, or to forsake him. To repent of our sins, or to harden our hearts. To remain in the Church and the path toward salvation, or to fall away.

Also, might the more individualistic tone some read into Paul's words better reflect the personal angle the apostle mentions in the second paragraph—"We ... *who were the first*"? Certainly, the very first generation of believers—especially those who knew Jesus personally and lived with him—must have felt they had been specially and individually blessed, not just to have the general salvation all Christians share through Jesus, but to be among the actual few—in all of human history— who had seen and lived with the God-man while he was on earth.

Initially, I was unaccustomed to hearing these verses from Ephesians preached from a perspective of predestination. Perhaps, had I been brought up with an outlook of election ingrained within me, I would have a different but equally passionate belief regarding salvation that is still Christian in nature. I might also place more emphasis on God's sovereignty than on his justice, love, and mercy. More emphasis on thankfulness for my existence as a Christian and more comfort in thinking God has an eternal plan for me as an individual, instead of emphasizing my human will and the need to make my own personal, daily decisions to move myself closer and closer to God.

To my Catholic ears, it logically follows that emphasizing God's sovereign choice at the expense of our human (yet God-given) decisions to cooperate in the Spirit's call to follow or deny Christ leads not only to God choosing the elect, but also the un-elect (the damned or "reprobate"). If he chooses some individuals from all eternity for the bliss of heaven, then he must also have chosen other individuals, through no specific fault of their own, for eternal damnation. Through his all-powerful nature he chooses outcomes for us that can clearly considered to be unfair and unjust.

Then Why the Debate?

Like all good children, we bristle when someone denigrates the attributes of our Father.

While the theory of election and predestination might attack the view of God being just and merciful and loving, the good people and faithful Christians who believe these doctrines have been taught to consider anything less than God's predestined election to save individuals once-for-all to be an attack on God's "Godness." How can we, they ask, choose to believe in salvation through faith in Christ if the Father has already predetermined our eternal damnation, or chose to deny Christ if the Father has already chosen us for eternity in heaven? Either possibility, they maintain, requires God to be either not all-powerful or not all-knowing. They feel those who don't believe in predestined election insult God's strength or wisdom, his sovereignty and omniscience.

So, let us take a step back and understand that neither side approaches these arguments with the desire to
insult our God, but to protect our God from perceived
slander.

For me, my concern was always this: if from the
beginning of time all who are saved were chosen to be
saved by the Father, no matter what, did Jesus come to
earth in vain? If the Father predestined me for eternal
bliss or torment, then he could have decided I am saved
or damned simply because I have gray hair, or bad breath,
or speak Spanish. Why would Jesus need to come to us
at all? Why did he have to provide us his example of true
humility or endure the pain of crucifixion? Do believers
in predestination insult God's mercy and justice? Do they
call into question the very reason for the Incarnation?

Personally, I do not find a warrant in scripture nor
can I accept in logic that an all-loving God and Father
would tell his Son, "Son, I want you to become a human,
suffer a horrible execution, and die completely separated
from me. We already know which souls we are going to
spend eternity with, so your life and death won't change
anything. Those who we have not elected won't praise
us for our glory or your sacrifice, as they will be cast
into hell. Those we have already elected to save won't be
happy with us or glorify us either when they see their
loved ones cast into hell, having never had a chance or
choice to avoid damnation in the first place."

I can, however, envision this conversation: "Son,
we love all our children but they won't *humble* themselves unless they see you humble yourself completely;
they won't *love* us unless they see your ultimate loving

sacrifice for them; they won't have *faith* in us unless they see me physically reflected in you; and they won't have *hope* unless your atonement gives all of them at least the chance to repent and spend eternity with us."

But what if we can be saved at one moment but not saved at another, as I've heard many Calvinistic Evangelical preachers ask? This is one of the fears that supports their insistence on predestination. If Jesus died for us and sent his Spirit to us, and we become "new creatures" when we believe in him (with God the Father being the one who called us to that faith in the first place), does Christ or the Holy Spirit or God the Father mean anything if we humans have the power to turn all their plans and intentions upside down and choose to deny their call to heaven?

Those who hold with predestination think that those of the opposite view believe "works" alone save us; we therefore have both the ability to save or to un-save ourselves without regard to Christ, depending upon what we do. Because of this, they fear we insult the Father's power, his sovereign will, and the sacrifice of the Son. If we can save ourselves, we have no further need or gratitude for Christ.

But I have lived all my Catholic life without once failing to thank God for Christ's life, his call for me, his sacrifice and his example. I may have to fight and claw my way to the gates of heaven, but I know the gates are unlocked only because of Jesus. I am biblically called to act, to *love* God with all my heart, mind and soul, but still I know that I love and worship God in his sovereign glory. I am subject to his will; I even ask daily that "thy will be done." He is my Lord and I need to obey. Even after coming to faith, I still feel the tug and allure of doubt, of lust, of pride, of sin, so I am always grateful the Father sent his Spirit to keep me from turning away from the narrow path. I am always dependent upon his aid and grace.

For me, then, believing in predestination means believing in an unfair, arbitrary, unmerciful and unloving God. But I realize most who believe in personal election reconcile their view by insisting that God is in fact merciful, just, and loving. It is just that God choses to express these traits only to a small group of individuals eternally chosen to receive his blessings.

My main concern is if those outside of the elect have been created by God with no choice but to deny him and endlessly sin, how can God hold us responsible for those sins? The answer was crystallized for me recently while listening to a leading Evangelical pastor who, explaining why his belief in election does not mean God is unjust or arbitrary, said (essentially echoing God's point in the final chapters of the Book or Job), *God is God so who are we to object?* This pastor said, "God is sovereign, and in his sovereignty, he's made us responsible for what we do."

At this, three things came to mind instantly. First, we see throughout history that sovereign, powerful, and capable kings or rulers have little need to control their subjects' every movement, thought, and attitude. Sovereigns who need to control everything are no longer sovereign at all; they are tyrants.

Second, let's take examples of this pastor's notion of God's sovereignty to their logical extreme: A parent who forces his son to get drunk, and then grounds him for driving under the influence. Or a general who commands a foot soldier to kill his unarmed prisoners, and then court-martials the young warrior for doing what he was commanded.

No one would consider such a parent or general to be fair, just, or merciful.

Finally, I thought of the explanation C.S. Lewis offers in *Mere Christianity*. One of his proofs for the existence for God is that God placed his nature of love, fairness, and mercy within us. All of us understand and share a common understanding of fairness, in which either side of any argument can claim a higher standard of right and wrong, a standard that has obviously come from, and reflects, God.

Isn't that standard of fairness at the foundation of Jesus' command to love one's neighbor? That we are to want the best for them, that we are to be fair to them, that we are to offer them mercy? Christ tells us to do these things because he has given us the wisdom to understand and the strength to carry them out. Understanding and desiring fairness cannot be in our nature unless it is first in the nature of our God. Yet the theology of predestination reflects a God who is inherently unjust, unfair, unmerciful, and in the end unloving.

Concerning notions of salvation, I recognize the logic and sincerity in both Catholic and Evangelical beliefs and consider both to be truly Christian. Although these conflicts cannot justify divisive anger, there are five practical reasons why this issue is important to both perspectives.

1. Establishing that only a "chosen" few are to be saved generates a natural prejudice against those who we see as not being "chosen," just as Old Testament Jews maintained distance from Gentiles. Catholics (see *Catechism*, 841) teach that many faiths hold at least a kernel of God's truth; that in ways we do not know God is working to open a path for those who in faith and humility choose to return home to him.

2. Deemphasizing the need to live godly lives and cooperate with God's call for eternal salvation—a natural outcome of believing we are either elect or reprobate for reasons beyond our influence or control—leads us to believe we do not need to keep learning about God, repenting of our sinful nature, and following Jesus.

3. Predestination provides an image of God that is difficult to explain to non-believers and doesn't match the God of justice and mercy portrayed in scripture.

4. Personal predestination puts into question Jesus' reason for coming to earth. If we are already chosen from all time, then why would Jesus need to sacrifice himself? His example would not matter. His atonement would make no difference, since the Father already decided who would be saved. Christ's Church and the Bible would not matter either, for again, if we have already been chosen for salvation the Bible and Church can add or subtract nothing with regards to our destiny.

5. We are led to mistaken views on issues such as forgiveness, justification, and salvation. We do

not need to forgive others or ourselves, for if we
are "chosen," God has already determined we are
forgiven, justified, and saved. If we are not part of
the elect, we can never be forgiven, justified, or
saved.

As I wrestled with this final point regarding forgiveness, I considered many examples from scripture.
Jesus told Peter, for example, to forgive his brothers seventy times seven times. He did not say, "You have already
forgiven your brother once-for-all when you became
my follower, as I have forgiven you once-for-all, so you
do not have to forgive him again." Jesus also taught the
apostles the Lord's Prayer, which eloquently commands
that we never cease asking for, and providing others
with, forgiveness. In fact, in this prayer Jesus gives the
almost terrifying command that God's forgiveness of our
sins will follow "as" we forgive our fellow sinners. This
prayer, the only one in scripture given by Jesus himself,
was important enough to be mentioned in two Gospels,
Matthew and Luke. The evangelists phrase the context of
the story to make clear this was an actual prayer, not just
a few words Jesus offers as a pattern of how to pray well.
The Lord did not say, "Well, pray something like this…"

These Gospels not only note that Jesus said the
prayer but recorded them as Jesus' own words. The prayer
must also have been in common use when the Gospels
were written and remained so through the fourth century
when the New Testament Canon was acknowledged.
Writing at the turn of the fifth century, Saint Augustine,
for one, took great pains to review this prayer line-by-line.

Evangelicals often cite Saint Augustine to support concepts such as the preservation of the saints and total depravity. Augustine, however, wrote to combat heretics (Pelagius and his followers) who taught that humans, entirely through their own will and efforts, can lead a life holy enough to merit heaven. This doctrine also can imply that Christ came for no reason. In truth, however, Catholic Christians who do not accept personal predestined election typically are not Pelagian; not believing in predestination does not mean believing that humans can save themselves. They fully understand that without Christ, without his sacrifice, without his example and his Spirit, human beings can never be reconciled with the Father. In a similar way, in a *practical* way, those who promote predestination and election do not actually believe our lives, actions, thoughts, and attitudes do not affect our eternal destiny.

The meaning of Christ's role in our salvation might be visualized by picturing heaven as a safe city within a dark and dangerous forest. We are all born outside this city, the descendants of citizens whose rebellion brought about their exile. However, singing from within the city walls echoes through the forest. All the forest dwellers have seen—or at least have heard of—scouts sent out from this city. These messengers invite all who listen to who put aside their rebellious ways and follow them back onto a path the king of the city cut through the woods to guide them home. Some decide not to follow that path, some make it onto that path and then—out of weariness or desperation, or the preference to remain behind with friends, or the choice to follow a different path that seems more likely to lead to the City—leave the straight way or turn back or just sit down where they are.

Some, however, do stay on the path or at least return to it every time they wander off course. At the great gate in the wall of the city, they discover that long ago the Prince of the city himself opened the once-locked gate. It was he who first went out and blazed the safe path through the forest. He personally cleared it, going deep into the forest until rebels fell upon him and killed him. Those who have chosen to reject their rebellion and make it to the gate are invited to stay safely within the city forever.

A writer witnessing this city and those who come to it can rightly describe those who made it to the gate as being "predestined" to live safely within the city eternally. To honor the sacrifice of the prince, the king determined never to lock the gate again, and never to turn away those who chose to travel along the prince's path.

But this form of predestination does not imply any single soul within the forest—all of whom at least have heard the echoes of singing from the city—had been denied a chance and a choice to find the path and enter through the gate. All of us—whether we made it to the walls of the city after following the straight path, or whether we made it to the walls after a long and lonely struggle through the perilous wood—all of us also had the choice to turn aside and decline the city. The king offers the salvation of the city to all; he sends messengers to help us journey through the forest; but he does not send out his armies to seize people and bring them to the city as captives.

As I mentioned earlier, our first response to a new or unfamiliar view of Christian theology may be to consider its adherents as insincere or illogical. Only after listening to both sides of issues like those we have discussed and truly understanding each other's beliefs can the logic on both sides be appreciated. Logic, of course, is not the same as correctness. Every legal case has two sides. Both have the same evidence and legal expertise to develop a story, the one supporting a verdict of innocence often just as logical as one supporting a guilty verdict. The losing team is not necessarily illogical; in fact, their argument may have been better developed than the other. Their loss may be due to the jury's interpretation of their arguments.

An analogy for predestination Evangelicals like to use illustrates their logic. We are all, they say, in a lake drowning in our sins. We can't swim, the analogy holds, at least not well enough to get to shore so unless we are saved we will drown. Jesus comes along in a rowboat and pulls us out of the water. He alone chooses who to pull out. He alone does all the work. He alone saves. It is impossible, the analogy suggests, that Jesus would bring some into the boat and then throw them out again.

But such logic does not ensure a proper conclusion.

We used *The Godfather* and *The Apostle* to illustrate important points. Let's evaluate this analogy through the lens of another movie, *Titanic*. At the end, the surviving crew of the doomed ship row their life boats through a maze of helpless, freezing bodies.

If Jesus was one of those crew members rowing through that bitter sea, surrounded by dozens of his beloved children struggling to survive in the frigid waters, can we envision him (as the predestinational position holds), plucking one sinner out of the water but rowing past another? It is one thing to think of Jesus as a hands-off God-spirit bestowing his grace to one person while rejecting another. It's quite a different thing—and probably much more true to life—to envision an actual Jesus inches away from his desperate brothers and sisters, his beloved creations, hearing their horrible cries for help, feeling their hands beat against the sides of his life boat, seeing the terror in their eyes as they realize they will certainly die without his help, yet simply rowing past them.

Does that mean he has to lift all the people into his boat, even those who don't like him and are swimming away? No, he can lovingly desire that everyone make it into the boat without forcing them to accept his help. We still must swim toward him, or at the very least reach out to grab his open hand. Those who die do so because they have rejected him. And, once in the life-boat, we still possess the human will that allows us to jump back into the frozen waters.

Previously, we discussed sola fide, faith in Christ alone. In the spirit of Christian unity as well as effective interfaith dialogue, let me add one more point. Predestined election assumes God pre-selected some to be saved. The chosen are given faith in Christ, and only through this faith are sins forgiven. But if heaven is open only to those forgiven through faith in Christ, what about people who lived before Christ or had not heard of Jesus because he had not yet been born? Can anyone in such a state receive forgiveness?

Some who lived before Jesus, who never knew him or claimed forgiveness through their faith in him have indeed been saved. In his sovereignty, justice, and mercy God allowed Moses and Elijah into heaven. We know this since they were with Jesus at the Transfiguration. We know Abraham, Isaac, and Jacob also are with the Father in heaven, since Jesus used them as a case-in-point to the Jewish leaders that there is life after death (Mt 22: 31-32). And, David? What about the "man after God's own heart," the king whose throne Jesus has assumed for all eternity? Even though he committed grave sins— lying, adultery, and murder—and had never met, seen, or heard of Jesus of Nazareth, he surely has reached heaven. A man not predestined to be saved through faith alone in Christ, yet nonetheless saved.

So, if some born before Jesus still have been saved through God's mercy, might this also apply to those who had never heard of Jesus due to geography, or whose only experience with Jesus has been warped due to culture, family, or politics?

Of course, when dealing with non-believers, Christians should profess and proclaim humankind's total reliance upon Jesus. We might be more effective bringing others to Christ, however, if we don't condemn people and their cultures as "un-elect" (or "reprobate"). Some believe evangelization to the unsaved world will be effective only if non-believers are told there is no other way to God and that through such evangelization we cooperate with God's plan to bring back to himself his predetermined elect. To me, however, the idea of God already having elected one remnant (and one remnant only) for salvation does not motivate me to reach out to non-believers. What motivates me is the possibility of cooperating with God's plan to reach out to *all* people, no matter how "un-electable" we believe them to be.

Friends on Both Sides

There is a saying, "I have friends on both sides of this argument, and I stand by my friends." In some arguments concerning doctrine, our friends on either side are not that far apart, and unity between Christians may not depend on one side or another "giving in" and going against what they have been taught as on understanding the other side's position more fully. Forty years after Luther sparked the Reformation and the development of Protestant concepts like predestination and election, the Council of Trent declared the following:

> It is furthermore declared that in adults the beginning of that justification must proceed from the predisposing grace of God through Jesus Christ, that is, from His vocation, whereby, without any merits on their part, they are called; that they who by sin had been cut off from God, may be disposed through His quickening and helping grace to convert themselves to their own justification by freely assenting to and cooperating with that grace; so that, while God touches the heart of man through the illumination of the Holy Ghost, man himself neither does absolutely nothing while receiving that inspiration, since he can

also reject it, nor yet is he able by his own free will and without the grace of God to move himself to justice in His sight. (Session VI, Chapter V)

By the mid-1500s, in response to claims by Luther and his followers regarding issues such as justification, the Catholic Church restated its agreement with many of the points they raised. In response to the Reformers' issuing new challenges and requesting new definitions concerning key issues such as justification, Trent provided more precise terminologies and doctrines.

Yet now, five hundred years later, Christian denominations still preach against each other even though the Council of Trent established a possible bridge of reconciliation.

Why?

Having listened to and studied this issue for over a decade within the Evangelical environment, I believe the issue comes down to this. In general, Evangelicals believe that if through our human will we are involved *at all* with our regeneration and salvation, it means we believe we are saved *entirely* through our own actions, and we can then claim credit for our "works." We might then consider ourselves saved without returning proper gratitude to God or demonstrating humility before his sovereignty.

As stated at Trent, however, Roman Catholics believe God calls us, prods us, "quickens" us, provides his Word and his Church for us and regenerates us in baptism. Ultimately, however, he respects human will, allowing us to decide whether to follow and love him and, if we sin again, return to Christ through repentance. Just as at the Jordan River John the Baptist called the people to decide for themselves to repent, just as Jesus repeatedly asked his listeners (including St. Peter when they first met in Peter's boat) to repent and come back to God, the Father's sovereign will *is* for us to come back to him in love, freely and without coercion. If we accept our weakness and our love for and reliance upon God, then the Father, his Son and his Spirit enter us as we reclaim our spiritual lives.

But, is it Biblical?

Over and over my children and I hear in our Evangelical churches, "What does the Bible say?" Catholic doctrine says we are saved by and through God's sovereign plan, a plan that respects for our own human will and our decisions regarding repentance and faith. It is stated clearly in the Catechism, which in turn grew out of a two thousand-year-old tradition dating back to the apostles. But is it clearly laid out in the Bible?

Evangelical sermons often cite the Bible to support individual justification and salvation as God's one-time predetermined choice for certain individuals. For example, Psalm 75:7 states: "But it is God who executes judgement, putting down one and lifting up another." For many Evangelicals, such phrases are taken to mean God chooses to bless (to lift up to heaven) some people and not others.

I am concerned when Christians, regardless of denomination, insist certain scriptures were written for the early Church or for people in Old Testament times and are no longer valid. For example, some claim that what Paul wrote about not allowing women to preach before men this statement conveyed Christ's desire for the Church universally, while others consider this directive to be addressed to a specific group of followers in a specific culture at a specific time, and not necessarily for the modern world. Others disapprove of doctrines drawn naturally from sources such as the Letter of James and preach that James was written only for the Jews, whereas Paul was writing to the Gentiles (and somehow all Christians today should consider themselves Gentile and therefore follow only Paul).

Still, considering that all of scripture is inspired and can be universally helpful, if not universally applied, let's look again at Psalm 75. When interpreting the verse, the various definitions of "blessing" must not be confused. In the days of Jacob, Moses, and the rest, God cursed or blessed (brought down or lifted up) the Jewish people as a nation in terms of land and prosperity and victory in battle. In that era, in that part of the world, blessing one nation (giving the Hebrews the land of Canaan, for example) meant cursing another (Canaanites). It was a zero-sum world, the size of the pie fixed; it only mattered who received the larger piece.

But in the New Testament, blessing is not a zero-sum game. After Christ, *blessing* came to refer to personal and eternal salvation. God's offer of this "blessing" is *infinite*. God did not create a fixed number of souls to save and does not arbitrarily decide to bless Brandi Smith by giving her the seat in heaven that could have been claimed by Anthony Johnson. God wants all his children to join him in heaven. In interpreting "blessing" and conversely the opposite—eternal damnation—as the "curse" from the psalm, Old Testament verses should not be applied out of context. The meaning of "blessing" in the old covenant is different from the new.

In controversy, the middle ground may not always the correct position, but in this area of theology, perhaps it is. Living as both a Catholic and Evangelical Christian, I remind myself God is sovereign, and I owe him everything, including the gift of Jesus in my life and the fact I've been born into a time, culture, and family that have brought me to this Christian faith. But I believe a just and merciful God has left it at least partially in my hands to accept his grace and cooperate with him in living a faithful, Christ-like life.

On the way to work I used to listen to Colin Smith, an Evangelical radio preacher whose Irish accent was pleasant to listen to and whose teaching I often found insightful. One morning he spoke about Christian beliefs regarding justification, what he deemed "one of the major differences between Catholics and Evangelicals." He said, "Let me be as fair as I can. The Catholic view is that justification is something earned over time, while Evangelicals believe it is given to a believer once-for-all. So, for Catholics it's like being given a spotless cloak to wear by Jesus when we come to faith, and then we must keep this cloak clean throughout our lives. Because of this—even the best of us can only be agnostic toward our salvation—that is, we do not know for sure whether we are saved (we don't know if our cloaks are clean enough)."

He then added: "Then they go through confession and repentance."

At first this pastor's argument seemed to acknowledge that Catholics and Evangelicals share the same bedrock idea of justification. The opening paragraph on justification in the *Catechism of the Catholic Church* states:

> The grace of the Holy Spirit has the power to justify us, that is, to cleanse us from our sins and to communicate to us "the righteousness of God through faith in Jesus Christ.... But if we have died with Christ, we believe that we shall also live with him. For we know that Christ being raised from the dead will never die again.... The death he died he died to sin, once for all, but the life we live he lives to God. So you also must consider yourselves as dead to sin and alive to God in Christ Jesus" [The quotation is taken from Romans 6:8-11]. (1987)

Some Evangelicals claim Catholics exaggerate the human role in salvation at the expense of God's glory and sovereignty. What Catholics really believe, however, is reflected in the *Catechism*, drawing upon the Council of Trent, which was called to address directly those doctrines the early Reformers saw separating Catholicism from the fundamental Christian faith taught by Jesus and his apostles:

When God touches man's heart through
the illumination of the Holy Spirit, man
himself is not inactive while receiving that
inspiration, since he could reject it; and yet,
without God's grace, *he cannot by his own free
will move himself toward justice in God's sight.*
(1993, italics added)

Catholics believe that throughout our lives our
own sinful choices and denials of Christ in fact do soil
our "spotless robes." Through the plan and grace of God,
we can repent, come back to Christ through personal
confession and the sacrament of reconciliation. By this
process, Jesus washes our cloaks clean once more. We
never presume God must allow us into heaven, but we
know we can return to the state of grace given us through
our initial justification.

Evangelicals often cite C.S. Lewis's *Mere Christianity*,
where he says that he, a long-time atheist, found one of
the main proofs of God in his own personal experience
of all men and women having common feelings concerning right and wrong, and in basic fairness. He noticed
even the most ardent atheists will still object if someone
cuts ahead of them in line, knowing that action to be
somehow unfair. But how, Lewis asks, can an action be
considered unfair unless there is some cosmic guide or
rule of fairness? The mere fact we all feel the existence of
a higher moral code proves the existence of whatever created the code. It proves that God exists. If someone cuts
in front of us in line, both the cutter and the cut-ee will
not argue over whether cutting in line is unfair—they

both believe it is—but over why in this case one or the other was justified in jumping the line.

So, too, I believe to our core we all *feel*—no, we all to our core *know*—the Catholic view of justification is correct. After first believing in Christ, we have all sinned many, many times. Despite receiving a spotless cloak at our moment of faith and justification, unless we have grown terribly hard of heart, we understand that our new sins or denials of Christ's call make things "not right" with our Lord, that we are somehow separated from our Savior and our God. At some moments we all wonder if we have failed too greatly for God to forgive us. In fact, the more deeply we grow to love God during our journey of faith, the more troubled we become at even the smallest transgression against our Father's will.

In that moment, if we believe our initial forgiveness and justification came through faith in Christ, why is it strange that the same process and the same faith and the same act of repentance, offered toward the same Savior, again and again brings us back to a state of saving grace after our new failures?

We must repent, turn from our sins and ask for forgiveness the first time we come to Christ. Don't we all understand intrinsically the truth behind the proposition that we need to repent again, turn from our sins again, and again ask for forgiveness to be right with God once more after we fall? We then will have rewashed our cloaks. More importantly, the human being beneath our cloak, if still not yet perfect, is at least placed once again upon the correct path toward holiness.

Returning to the question that began this section, is the Catholic view biblical? Do we have to return to Christ after we sin, and do we need to maintain and grow our faith after our initial justification?

Over the past decade my Evangelical faith family has challenged me to read the Bible with much more attention to detail. In the Book of Revelation, Jesus' words to the seven churches describe those who once were strong in the faith but have begun to fall away. Jesus reminds these believers of their possible damnation should they not repent anew and return to God. Elsewhere, Saint Paul admonishes his readers to not "make shipwreck" of their faith, and to move beyond the baby's milk of their initial faith toward the solid food of their beliefs. The same apostle wrote about the Eucharist, about studying the Word to maintain and build our faith, and about the process of repentance. John the Baptist told the "vipers" who came to him at the Jordan to demonstrate true repentance and sanctification before he would baptize them. Jesus told the woman he saved from stoning, "Go and from now on do not sin anymore."

Most of all, the prayer Jesus taught his disciples commands us to ask the Father without ceasing to "forgive us our trespasses as we forgive others."

The Moral Dilemma of Conversion

Once I understood that Evangelicals and Catholics alike can be saved, my time within the Evangelical Church became more comfortable and beneficial. I grew to understand that the lingering distrust between our expressions of the faith is based largely upon misconceptions or mis-definitions, some of them centuries old. I understood our passions come not from un-Christian anger at each other, but from very Christian desires to protect the attributes of a God we try to love with all our hearts, minds, and souls. But I still harbored a concern as I sat with my children at Evangelical services, sometimes exposing us to aggressively anti-Catholic sentiments. What then about our attempts to "convert" one another?

During my Catholic upbringing, I rarely, if ever, heard a Catholic—clergy or lay person—assert a moral imperative to "convert" non-Catholic Christians to Catholicism. Are we all to reach out to unbelievers with the gospel? Of course! It is every Christian's duty to do so in a humble, loving way. Are we to express those things within Catholicism we believe might benefit non-Catholic Christians? Of course. But, should we try to destroy fellow Christians' faith in the hope of bringing them to Catholicism?

No.

I have not witnessed the same restraint, unfortunately, within Evangelical churches. From my first service, I saw and heard about repeated attempts to "convert" and "save" Catholics. Usually this came in the form of "missionary" trips to largely Catholic countries (most commonly, Latin America) that yielded a great number of "conversions" and "salvations." I realized part of every dollar I gave to these churches was used not to promote the growth of the Christian church among unbelievers, but to weaken and destroy one of the Church's fundamental parts. This "cross-conversion" undermines

Christ's plan for his church, and if not done with the utmost care, is immoral.

Why?

At a cursory level, of course, such "family bickering" confuses non-believers about the sincerity and integrity of all Christians. If we claim that those who profess their belief in Jesus, God the Son, receive salvation through faith in this Christ, why would one group of Christ-followers ever consider another group to be damned? It is a great hypocrisy. Such actions demonstrate a belief that salvation comes not from faith in Christ, but only through a faith and set of practices exactly like our own. Then, every time the understanding of that faith changes, we separate from yet another group who had previously been our brothers and sisters but now are considered unsaved and on the road to damnation. Thus, over the past five centuries the Reformation has engendered hundreds if not thousands of denominations, each suspicious of the other, and all suspicious of Catholics. How can Christians who claim other Christians are lost or even evil explain God's truth to non-Christians?

On a more personal level I see a deeper evil at work, a more sinister trap for the unwary. Those who seek to "convert" someone from one Christian faith to another must do more than start a conversation and introduce new concepts. The converter must first destroy the other Christian's existing faith to create a spiritual vacuum, to be filled with their preferred form of Christianity. In doing so, however, the converter puts into jeopardy the soul of a person who previously believed in and trusted Christ. A few of those approached for conversion may find their first faith destroyed and replaced with the new, but an equal or larger number lose their faith altogether.

To bring about such "conversions," one Christian must make another Christian believe that the truth of their faith-life is false, that their church culture is false, that the parents and relatives who had inculcated them in their faith were either stupid or liars. Many will wonder, "How can I ever trust in any faith again?" When told that the faith they were born into, the faith taught and believed by their family and friends, is false or even evil, many then reject all Christian churches, all claims of truth, and any relationship with God.

All for what? For a few who would successfully "convert" from one form of saving belief in Christ to another? Yes, and little more. A 2014 survey of those who had recently left the Catholic faith showed three times as many becoming "unaffiliated" than becoming Evangelical. Three times as many left Christianity altogether than converted to a different Christian expression of the faith. How many of these ex-Christians lost their faith, at least in part, because of the challenges and attacks coming from other Christians?

At our Evangelical church a couple of years ago, a guest pastor spoke about missions. He clicked through a PowerPoint presentation that listed America as having 300+ million people and "60 million Jesus followers." Mexico had 100+ million people, and only 9 million "Jesus followers," and on and on throughout other countries including Egypt, where he listed "practically zero" Jesus followers. This presenter was not a lay person presenting a personal interpretation of facts, but a trained pastor, responsible for bringing unbelievers to Christ. Yet his slides did not count most Christians, especially Catholics, among true Christ-followers at all.

He also excluded the Egyptian Coptic Christians who that very weekend had been martyred by the dozens because they were Jesus followers. To him, "following Jesus" meant following his style of Evangelical Christianity; all other "Christians" were not Christians at all.

Adding or Multiplying

Should all Christians then blindly accept the faith of their birth and not listen to or interact with those who have different experiences with Christianity? Since every faith is different in some way, is one faith "better" than all the others? What would a "best" faith include? Ideally, the most "fundamental" element would be aligning closely with the will of Jesus. But since opinions concerning his will differ, a more objective aspect of the "best" faith would be a church that has endured and grown across multiple cultures, a church that transmits its faith consistently and faithfully to each new generation, a church that maintains the faith of the elderly as they move closer to eternity. These, among others, are the "fundamental" traits of a successful church.

When a person of faith faces the need to take his children to a different church, to risk the "fundamental" foundation for their growing souls, much less one's own soul…. when challenged by a spouse who no longer believes that the faith community into which you were born—in my case the Catholic Church—truly represents the fundamental path to life, this issue becomes critical.

Like most religious people, I have a deep bond with my faith; like most Catholics I believe my faith is the key to bringing up our children. Should I then fear going to another "Christian" church? Don't I believe that all Christians can be saved? All Christian faiths do indeed share a good deal of the truth, and from my personal experience Evangelicals, especially, are close in terms of practical theology with my Catholic family. My fellow Evangelical churchgoers are good people with whom I hope to spend eternity.

So, why do I still feel uneasiness in my gut? Deep down, even after these past thirteen years of "dual-citizenship," I still have questions not so much concerning whether Evangelicals can be saved, but whether my children, brought up partially in that culture and practice, will maintain their faith throughout their lives and enter God's eternity.

In the end, this is *the* question. For those you love most deeply, it is the *only* question—am I doing what will bring my children to eternal fellowship with Christ? Do I feel that following the Catholic path is right? Even if my family can be saved by following the Evangelical path can I—should I—gently and lovingly still point my children back toward the fullness of truth I believe is found in the Catholic faith?

At this point I would like to tell my children they can be saved as any type of Christian; in other words, they can come to the right answer even if not in the same way I have. It is like a child learning that you can use four fingers to count to four, and later that you can get to four by adding two plus two. Learning addition gets the same right answer as counting on their fingers, though it is easier. I would remind them, however, that soon after they learn addition, their teachers show them how to multiply. The world is not simple, and neither are the questions we face. When asked what eight times twelve hundred is, my children will learn it is easier to multiply the two numbers than to add eight to itself twelve hundred times. Multiplication offers greater surety of a right answer. When we learn multiplication, we do not go back to addition; and once we know multiplication, we do not allow our children to end their training at addition. St. Paul wrote to his readers who obviously had come to basic faith in Christ that they were only being nourished at that point by baby's milk, and they needed to go deeper into their faith.

So, it is not sinful to tell a Christian of another denomination that we consider our view of the faith to be the most appropriate, as long as we don't tell them their trust in Christ is invalid and even evil because they are still trying to use addition while we are using multiplication.

Most important is becoming and remaining Christian. It is important to choose the "right" Christian path, to follow God in the way most appropriate for maintaining our Christianity and maximizing our productivity for the goals of his kingdom. We who feel we have found the right path need to explain it and espouse it, though with a humility that does not threaten the core beliefs of our fellow Christ-followers and risk their leaving the faith altogether.

Seeing Beyond

From a layman's perspective, I offer another insight born from living within two Christian families and listening to the differences in language. Evangelicals trace their origins to the Reformation. The forefathers in their expression of the faith (Martin Luther and others), faced one overriding task—to show the tasks or works within the Catholic expression of faith were unnecessary, perhaps even damaging. From this need developed a theology of justification by faith alone (no tasks required to start in the faith), and justification once-for-all (no tasks required to continue in the faith).

Catholics also believe in *justification* (forgiveness) through faith in Christ. In fact, early in the Reformation, the Council of Trent reiterated:

> If anyone saith, that man may be justified before God by his own works, whether done through the teaching of human nature, or that of the law, without the grace of God through Jesus Christ; let him be anathema. (Canon I)

Catholics, however, understand that initial justification is not enough. God commands that we build and grow in our faith, a process called sanctification. The process of sanctification requires effort, "work," be it continual study and meditation on the Word of God or works of charity or mercy. Sanctification is not once-for-all, but a process. Now, there is no set standard of sanctification we must reach, no checklist whereby the Church confirms a person to be automatically saved without an ongoing relationship with Christ. The process of sanctification does not eliminate the need of faith in Christ; rather, it seeks to perfect our faith in him. Sanctification helps us avoid the rocky shores that can, as St. Paul wrote, "make shipwreck of our faith."

This conforms with everyday experience. If we feel our spouse will be happy and our love and marriage will survive even if we do nothing more than attend the wedding ceremony, we are in for a rude awakening. A student beginning college needs to attend class and study or soon will be returning home to live in his parents' basement. If we begin a dream job and then just sit around we are likely to get fired. A soldier who chooses not to obey her superiors will soon be court-martialed or discharged.

Perhaps the analogy with military service is the most relevant to our considerations here. Before the end of the military draft in 1973, for example, some joined the armed forces willingly. Just as Evangelicals see an outside force (God) predestining (drafting) some to saving faith, the government would compel men into the armed services. Whether a volunteer or draftee, however, every soldier, sailor, aviator, or marine had to fulfill his or her tasks. All were required to complete boot camp, all needed to succeed in their specialized training. Those who refused were dishonorably discharged.

At the many Evangelical services and programs I have attended, I have never once heard the pastor say, "Well, now that everyone here has expressed faith in Christ, you are all justified for the rest of your lives, so this will be our last service." No. Every pastor encourages the faithful to attend services, read the Bible, do good works, ask for forgiveness if they've done something sinful, pray to the Father. Every pastor—on a practical level—understands that these ongoing works keep the flock on the road to Christ.

We are all on that same road together. We all seek Christ, for we are all Christian. Moreover, our goal (or requirement) to do good works and avoid sin is not about us. Our life in Christ is not, and cannot be, merely a personal relationship between us and our Savior. If we focus only upon what our faith life with Jesus does for us, we are being selfish. Jesus does not allow for selfishness; he instead formed a family out of his apostles and they a family of each following generation of believers. Our sanctification is not only for us; it is a necessary help for those in this family, this Kingdom of God.

Chapter 3

Scriptures

Love of Learning

All people are inclined to learn, but the Evangelical church has a particularly strong focus on teaching. In Evangelical churches, the worship services have the overtones of a college lecture hall (though with much more comfortable seats!). Evangelicals teach well because the entire atmosphere is set up for teaching. It is most important to teach the *right things,* of course, but it is hard to learn even the right things if not taught correctly and in the right environment.

The first Evangelical congregation we attended was not a "mega" church. If I had gone to a megachurch first, I would have been turned off by the *seeming* lack of holiness due to worshiping in such a large, multi-purpose venue. The distraction of constant PowerPoint presentations where the greatest power of all is supposed to point us toward heaven would have been disturbing. The first, smaller church was more intimate, and the congregation spent a good deal of time openly sharing life experiences. The pastors, both of whom seemed to have come from a Catholic background, led the church in prayers for the community, although they differed in form from the shared communal prayer I experience in the Catholic Mass.

The Evangelical service, however, was clearly focused upon preaching—the reading and explanation (exegesis) of a specific scripture passage. My fellow congregants, like good students, pulled out their pens and highlighters and took notes within their own bibles. In our second Evangelical church home, the megachurch, we encountered the same pattern, but its sheer size curtailed personal testimonies from the congregation. During each service we spent thirty to fifty minutes digging into one small group of verses, sometimes picking apart the words and meanings to greater depth than most of my college professors did with their various subjects; "unpacking" (to use the favorite term of the day) what the pastor believed the Holy Spirit wanted us to understand.

Seventy-Five Minutes

The Evangelical services introduced me to the shocking concept of "seventy-five minutes." It is almost a given that Catholic parishioners will self-destruct after sixty minutes (sometimes the fuse is set at forty-five or fifty if they are attending the last Mass of the day during football season). After receiving the Eucharist, some parishioners (including myself on occasion, I must admit) head for the parking lots.

Theologically, we know that the Mass does not revolve around preaching. The Mass's effectiveness does not depend upon the skill of the homilist. It includes the "liturgy of the Word," but Catholics are equally or more focused upon the Eucharist. However, the beautiful and powerful event of receiving the Lord should not prevent or limit a full and powerful expression of the liturgy of the Word as well.

Soon after we stopped watching Sesame Street, most of us grew beyond the limitation of a fifty-minute classroom setting. We spend eight hours or more each day at work, two hours sitting still watching a movie, three hours or more concentrating on a sporting event. Perhaps it is just *barely* possible, and maybe even beneficial, for us to stay in one place in the presence of our God for more than an hour each week—maybe even for a full seventy-five minutes. At Mass, we join in a two thousand-year-old way of Christian life that should affect every part of our individual experiences, and to seek the future relationship with God that determine our eternal destiny as well.

Should we not be able to survive for seventy-five minutes?

Now, in addition to the Liturgy of the Word, the Mass is an experience of the Eucharist, a union and remembrance and celebration of what Christ did for us. Though the Mass was never meant to be a classroom or pep rally, in today's world we shouldn't restrict the Mass in terms of what it can and should be. It can and should present, in part, ongoing instruction in life and our faith. The Mass is not only a *culmination*, but also a *starting point* from which we move more deeply into the Christian faith. An alpha and an omega.

In the allotted five to ten minutes of a typical Catholic homily, it is impossible to generate an emotional connection to what's being taught. Above and beyond the emotional impact of the sermon, the intellectual depth concerning a subject relating to eternal life simply requires more time. I know many who think that a celibate priest cannot present an in-depth homily that explores the shared life experience of most parishioners without "stepping in it."

But I disagree.

Most people do not need or prefer an emotionally-laden, "I'm one of you and understand your pain" sermon; they want to be nourished with the important "solid food" of our faith (as St. Paul said in 1 Cor 3:2). We want something we can *really* believe in; we want logical explanations supporting Christianity, specifically Catholicism, something that will last beyond lunch following the Mass and even beyond the Sunday afternoon football game. We want something we can later think about and use to justify, defend, explain, and live our faith as we face our workweek in a secular world.

Because Catholics generally end their formal faith training when they receive the sacrament of confirmation, many go no further in their studies than receiving eighth-grade explanations to eighth-grader questions. Later, when facing adult challenges to their faith from other adults, many cannot answer. We may know what is factually correct, but we cannot explain our faith in an adult context. We are trying to answer adult questions with a decades-old set of thirteen-year-old understandings. Weekly Mass is the only opportunity many Catholics have to grow in their faith as adults. The Mass must support this need.

And as for homilies needing emotional impact ... we may *feel* that we want a preacher who has experienced everything we have gone through, but we don't really *need* that. We may take comfort in hearing how our Evangelical pastor also battles the teenage angst of his children; but we may be inspired to hear the life story of a priest who has set aside all earthly possessions to serve us and Christ's Church. Whether from pastor or priest, it may be important for a church body to hear an individual's story, but it is far more important to learn the universal truths and stories of the faith lived out by millions of fellow Christians over the centuries.

We learn best through stories. Any priest or preacher can develop, learn or find great stories to illustrate any life experience, even those they haven't lived through personally. If they cannot, they can always look for guidance from the greatest story teller of all—Jesus Christ.

Catholics should not be afraid of the stories that make up our spiritual heritage, they are the greatest stories in all human experience. Paul himself said he wasn't a good speaker, yet by telling and re-telling the stories of our Lord he helped convert the world. Catholics should welcome the opportunity to sit still for an additional fifteen minutes once a week. We should reset our internal clocks and not be satisfied by a five-minute homily. Like our Evangelical brothers and sisters, we should be ready to learn—to really learn—about our Christian faith as adults.

How the Bible is Taught

Evangelicals have another advantage—they know and agree upon their own "rules." They might not know the history of the Bible, as we will discuss; they may not know the "traditional" interpretations of various verses; they may even maintain positions on certain issues that the Church fought over and decided a thousand years ago—but they do know their own internal rules.

They read the Bible. The preacher interprets what is read. They base most interpretations upon the Protestant "tradition" that began in the sixteenth century. They often use definitions of the Greek or Hebrew words found in early samples of the Bible as final arbiters to prove the validity of certain concepts, even if the definitions of these words themselves are best guesses or interpretations. They focus on Paul's writings, and they follow a path that includes verses found in Romans 8, Romans 9, John 3, Ephesians, Romans 1, etc.

They all know these rules.

Catholics commonly don't know the conventions of biblical study as well. Yes, we have other advantages: we appreciate the Eucharist, we recite and know the basic creeds of the Church, etc. But, in terms of the proper biblical study and a systematic reading in support of the basic doctrines of our faith, we don't know or follow the same set of rules.

We don't share the habit of reading the Bible beyond the readings at Mass. We don't know the history of the scriptures, and rarely are we taught the details concerning past heresies that have plagued the faith. We don't study the positive role the Church has played in maintaining orthodoxy and defining generally accepted Christian concepts such as the Trinity. We don't know the specific biblical verses that support our various sacraments. We don't know where to find information regarding issues such as the structure of the Church, the authority given to the apostles by the Lord, or how to explain Peter's role. At the same time, we have an unparalleled source of guidance and instruction that could support the topics of powerful Sunday homilies. Yet very few lay Catholics study the *Catechism of the Catholic Church*. In other words, we don't know or agree upon common approaches to properly study and deepen our faith.

Effective Catholic Christian preaching needs both interpretation of the written Word and an explanation of how these readings tie into church tradition, which elaborates and properly interprets the scriptures. We need to teach and learn how the various heresies of the past were overcome, how they sharpened true doctrine through their challenges and how, under different names, they continue to pop up today. We need to place scripture and the doctrines of the faith into proper and useful context by reflecting upon common, everyday spiritual life events we all share as seen through the *Catechism*. These should be our Catholic rules. We need to know them. We need to follow them.

Evangelicals study certain passages from scripture over and over. Catholics ought to do the same, guided by an easy-to-follow, systematic plan for bringing out the meaning behind the words. We should then tie the biblical texts to a common study of our interpretation of the faith as reflected in the *Catechism*. Just as Evangelicals follow their "rules" and can quote the same key chapters and verses from the Bible (i.e. "No one can see the kingdom of God without being born from above." [Jn 3:3].), so too, Catholics can benefit from knowing not only these biblical references but also what the *Catechism* teaches us about our faith. This combination of scripture and tradition was used to confront early heretics like Apollinarius (381 AD), who maintained that Jesus was God, but not truly man. Nearly 1700 years ago the Church acted to save Christians from this false teaching. In this case, we can understand from the scriptures that Jesus truly was a human being ("truly man"), reinforced by the *Catechism*: "The eternal Son also assumed a rational human soul" (471).

Evangelical preachers approach the written Word in a different way that I did in my Catholic experience. For example, at our megachurch we once spent forty minutes examining Jesus' comments as he entered Jerusalem. In Matthew 24, the Lord proclaims that those who flee to the hills when the city is attacked will survive. A minor point of scripture for sure, one I had read many times without much thought; but when put into historical context this fragment takes on a new level of meaning.

In our Evangelical sermon we lingered on this passage and learned that in Jesus' time, when trouble arose the standard practice was for people to seek protection by going *into* city strongholds. But Jesus instead tells his listeners to do the opposite, to *flee the city*. So, when the Romans came around the year 70 and laid siege to Jerusalem, most Jews ran into the city for safety, only to be killed. Those followers who remembered Christ's words and fled survived, eventually moving to the ends of the Roman world, planting the seeds of the first Christian churches.

I don't understand enough Greek to know whether the words ascribed to Jesus meant "to run to the hills," or simply "to seek shelter" when trouble came. The interpretation our pastor offered *could* in fact be totally wrong. Nevertheless, this level of investigation and explanation, if accurate, provides not only a point of great interest for the people in the pews, it also builds deeper trust in and appreciation of the Bible and what Jesus taught. Such detail reinforces the belief that statements and concepts within the core book of our faith are logical. Even if the pastor's interpretation of a certain biblical verse is mistaken, understanding there is a deep historical/logical explanation for what we read bolsters confidence. The more we compare what Jesus said with what would have been reasonable to contemporary listeners, the more we are comforted and inspired.

This Catholic approach of combining the Bible and the *Catechism*—the Word and tradition—can also allow a more balanced approach to difficult biblical passages. For example, Ephesians 5 presents how wives should submit to their husbands. Even though this passage can challenge an Evangelical preacher facing a contemporary audience of liberated women, reading the text in terms of its deeper meanings within the source languages allows for more flexibility and the opportunity to explain what St. Paul really meant. A superficial reading of, "Wives, be subject to your husbands" can lead to one view. But to go deeper and seek to tie in these comments with the passages that follow during a sermon longer than five to ten minutes allows the priest or pastor and their flock to consider that Paul's intent was not that wives must be subservient, but that all of us must humbly serve one another. In the following verses, men are commanded to love their wives not in the way that their contemporary culture expressed "love," but in the way Christ loved his Church—to the very point of dying for them.

Consider, for example, what *could* and *should* be learned from Catholic resources, what a priest could present if he used the *Catechism* as a resource to explain the world-wide, two-thousand-year-old testimony about the sacrament of matrimony. The *Catechism* states "marriage helps to overcome self-absorption, egoism, pursuit of one's own pleasure, and to open oneself to the other, to mutual aid and self-giving" (1609). This resource not only reflects upon what Paul wrote in Ephesians, but also upon the consistent teaching of the Church that for twenty centuries has faced questions and made distinctions about this most critical human relationship. When things get tough in marriage, for example, Catholics can consult not only the biblical texts but the *Catechism* which says in part:

> [Jesus'] unequivocal insistence on the indissolubility of the marriage bond ... could seem to be a demand impossible to realize ... but by coming to restore the original order of creation disturbed by sin, he himself gives the strength and grace to live marriage in the new dimension ... so that by following Christ,

> renouncing themselves, and taking up their
> crosses the spouses will be able to receive the
> original meaning of marriage. (1615)

A particular Bible passage may reflect a specific time and culture, so Catholics can judge contemporary practices against the living and effective rule of the faith as spelled out in the *Catechism*. When Paul writes that women should be quiet in church, for example, he may be reflecting the needs of the culture of his time. The *Catechism*, however, specifies that women should serve as lectors and distribute the Eucharist as lay ministers. By relying on the Bible as well as the tradition of the faith as represented by the *Catechism*, both clergy and laity can follow the same rules to discern how present practices conform with the tradition of the Church.

The New Testament

Any discussion concerning scripture must consider its origin and nature. It must address what is truly fundamental. I am a life-long active Catholic. I received after-school Catholic education until sophomore year of high school; as an adult I also took a crash course in Christianity at two Evangelical faith communities. For over forty years I have heard the three Bible readings at Mass each week, and for the past fifteen years I have listened almost every day to Evangelical and Catholic radio sermons based upon various Bible verses. Reflecting on my experience with scripture, however, I realize I received more direct instruction concerning the origins of the United States

Constitution, for example, than I have from any church regarding the origins of the Bible.

The Catholic faith survived a thousand-year dark age when few except the clergy knew how to read. Interpreting the Bible and developing instruction for the faith were left to experts. The results? For a millennium and a half such "experts" led the Church from being a fringe Jewish sect to the mainstream of Roman life (surviving against all odds as the Roman Empire collapsed), to strongly influence every aspect of life in medieval Europe. The Church confronted heresies that all contemporary Christians—Catholic, Protestant, and Evangelical—acknowledge, including some that endured even as long as the current split manifested in Protestantism that began five hundred years ago with the Reformation.

Many of these heresies developed through errant reading of scripture and misunderstandings concerning the tradition passed along by the apostles. Even today we see specific verses of scripture being used, for example, to deny the deity of Christ. This possibility led Catholics to be wary of over-emphasizing the Bible, especially after the Reformation, as a focus on the Bible felt too "Protestant." Not being brought up with a focus on scripture, in my experience, led many Catholics to fear that biblical study might lead to doubts concerning their faith or expose errors in Catholic practices. The history and development of the Bible, therefore, was deemphasized for Catholics.

Protestants also have a biblical blind spot caused by fear. In the Evangelical churches I have attended, emphasis is placed on the Bible, especially in their "tradition" of interpretation that began with Luther. Evangelicals sometimes reach beyond Luther to earlier church figures like Paul, Origen, Aquinas, and especially Augustine. In general, however, Evangelicals have a deep-seated reluctance to investigate the history of church tradition and the interpretation of specific scriptures prior to the Reformation. It almost seems that the Bible mysteriously "appeared" in Luther's time, and he read it his way while Catholics read it another. Evangelicals assume that the Bible presents all that is needed and acceptable concerning the fundamentals for doctrine, the formation of churches, and living a Christian life. But they ignore the fact that this understanding of the Bible's role has never been true before Luther. The Church never stepped back and said, "Let's look through the Bible and rebuild the faith only on what we read in those pages."

It seems obvious why Evangelicals largely fall silent concerning biblical history during the period between the apostles to the Reformation. When scholarship probes back beyond Luther toward the time when the New Testament scriptures were written and later accepted, history turns more and more Catholic. The Catholic Church has been consistent concerning doctrine and biblical texts, which by Luther's time both had existed for over a thousand years. Evangelicals who claim the authority of Augustine, or Aquinas, or even Paul or Peter must acknowledge that all these figures precede the Reformation. They lived within the early Church and (in the case or Paul and Peter) created and defined it. They believed in and taught and practiced (especially in the case of Aquinas and Augustine) those things that today would be considered part of the Catholic faith.

At one time, the Christian community had no scripture (by this I am referring to the uniquely Christian New Testament). Beginning at Pentecost, this era extended twenty-plus years between the resurrection and the first of Paul's recorded letters, then decades longer until the Book of Revelation was written. By the wisdom of Christ, the power of the Father, and the guidance of the Spirit, the pre-biblical Church established itself and began to spread throughout the world. Without a set of universally accepted texts, using oral accounts of what Christ said and did, this Church wrestled with and defined many major theological controversies. The apostles, upon the authority given to them by Christ and the unique vision given to Peter, made the most critical of these decisions: to accept into the Church Gentiles who would not need to follow Jewish laws, a decision, in other words, at odds with the understanding of the Old Testament scriptures at that time.

Three hundred years after this pre-biblical foundational era, several critical debates plagued the unity of the Church concerning issues that greatly affect our understanding of Christian truth today. Emperor Constantine called the church together to define what constituted acceptable Christian doctrine and what was to thereafter be considered heresy. Just as the apostles themselves did in Jerusalem when Peter and Paul determined it was valid to preach Christ to the Gentiles, this fourth century debate was decided through a church "council." Hundreds of bishops and other leaders met first at the Council of Nicaea, and then in the ecumenical council that followed in Constantinople. Their decisions shaped Christianity as we understand it today. Both Roman Catholics and Evangelicals accept the basic tenets of Christian faith, particularly concerning the Trinity, established at these councils.

Interestingly, the Protestant author of the massive work, *The Church Fathers*, Philip Schaff, stated his findings in terms of how the momentous decisions of these councils took place: "The question the Fathers considered was not what they supposed Holy Scripture might mean, nor what they, from a priori arguments, thought would be consistent with the mind of God, but something entirely different, to wit, what they had received. They understood their position to be that of witnesses, not that of exegetes." [6]

The critical issue at Nicaea was Jesus' identity and his relationship with the Father. Since the time of the resurrection, Christians had believed that Jesus was God the Son. Some leaders at Nicaea—faithful members of the church who relied upon the writings of the earliest Christians—came to believe differently. As the faith spread down through generations and into diverse cultures and backgrounds, the Church needed to define its true belief concerning this fundamental truth. Who was Jesus? From this debate came the Nicene Creed and the authoritative teaching on the nature of the Trinity.

Around this time church leaders also saw the need for a common set of scriptures upon which to support the faith, a semi-official "canon." Prior to Nicaea, many texts

---

6. *Nicene and Post-Nicene Fathers: Second Series, Volume XIV: The Seven Ecumenical Councils* (New York: Cosimo Classics), 2.

had been in widespread use by various local churches, but as Christianity grew it was necessary to determine which were to be considered universal, inspired, and holy. At Nicaea, Eusebius, a bishop who had studied under one of the great early church fathers, Origen, undertook the monumental task of writing the history of the first three hundred years or so of the Christian faith. He also gathered what the early Church considered the most trusted writings of the faith to debate and develop a New Testament canon.

The texts he considered authentic and inspired were those generally accepted and used by the major apostolic churches at Rome, Antioch, Jerusalem, and Alexandria. Eusebius and other early Church leaders like Irenaeus and Tertullian considered those churches to be primary because their bishops formed an unbroken chain of succession back to the apostles. Who better to understand the true meaning of Jesus' life? Who better to determine which writings reflected the Christian call? Of the more than one hundred writings considered, only twenty-seven—those included in the New Testament that Catholics and Evangelicals alike still use—were deemed true and inspired by the Holy Spirit.

So, the scriptures used today emerged through the inspired wisdom of the early church fathers. By the end of the fourth century, at the Synod of Carthage (397), the "Bible" as we know it was largely codified. For over eleven hundred years the "scriptura" Luther and his followers considered the sole source of faith had been shaped, treasured, and passed on by the Church of Rome.

What to Look Out For

Catholics may feel cautious or defensive when facing Evangelical conclusions regarding a specific interpretation of scripture, but few commonly held beliefs in Protestant theology suggest the need to differ with these brothers and sisters. They too are baptized into the Father, the Son and the Holy Spirit. And Catholics can take heart that when councils in the fourth and fifth centuries established the canon of the New Testament, nothing in those books was seen to contradict accepted theology and practice at that time.

Spending a decade within the Evangelical community, however, has made me realize several key practical concerns with Evangelical biblical interpretation. Although they interpret some sections of the Bible figuratively, as do other believers, Evangelicals often claim a more literal interpretation of scripture. Having been shaped by their particular expression of the faith, Protestants often do not recognize inconsistencies that are obvious to a Catholic like me who came from the outside into their worship services.

I am particularly concerned about "first and last things," the very beginning of the Bible (Genesis/creation) and its very end (Revelation/end times). In these two areas, many Evangelicals resist a figurative or allegorical interpretation. This is not an Evangelical "failure"; there are good reasons to weigh all evidence carefully before accepting a non-literal interpretation of any part of the Bible. From my childhood, I recall a Catholic priest's homily concerning the miracle of the multiplication of the loaves and fishes. The priest did not acknowledge the possibility that the event had a literal meaning. He claimed that when Jesus blessed and gave thanks for the few loaves and fish and then distributed this limited store of food to those around him, he simply provided his listeners an example to do the same. The food, the priest said, was always there, hidden in the crowd's knapsacks. The people surely would not be so foolish as to pursue Jesus into the wilderness without provisions. The vast amount of food "appeared" because the crowd followed Jesus' lead and shared what they had with others, not because of his miraculous power.

In advancing this concept, this priest did not consider that the gospel writers would not have recorded such an event had it happened due to normal circumstances. In its context and tone, the story *is* entirely about a miracle, about how the apostles experienced something well out of the ordinary. The text clearly says that the apostles were worried because the people had nothing to eat; they certainly did not believe that the people were hoarding what they had. The gospel writers either witnessed this miraculous multiplication of loaves and fish themselves or heard first-hand accounts from eyewitnesses. They present it as a true, historic fact. Indeed, Matthew 14 mentions that the disciples wanted Jesus to dismiss the crowds to secure food for the evening from the nearby towns. If the people were close enough to make it to these towns before nightfall, then why would they have been concerned about bringing food with them in the first place or asked to make a dangerous trek at the edge of darkness? By explaining this miraculous event in figurative terms, the priest reduced the holy to the mundane.

So, let us return to "first things." In the Evangelical churches, the consensus seems to be set on maintaining the literal truth of the creation narratives in Genesis. They interpret the story of Adam and Eve literally because for some believers, questioning the literal truth of *any* part of scripture opens the door of doubt concerning the entire Bible. Many bible stories, however, seek to explain a theological point more than to reflect literal truth. When I studied physics and engineering, every textbook used "models" to explain the attributes of nature in ways that we could understand, from the shape of the atom to the structure of a black hole. These models made the extraordinary understandable.

What points, then, are made by the story of Adam and Eve? God created human beings. God gave humans a will, which gives us the ability to obey or disobey. The first human beings used their will to disobey, a choice that continues as their descendants—all of us—repeatedly disobey God in our own lives. Our unity with God is broken and can only be restored by a Savior.

Is it *wrong* to believe in a literal Adam and Eve, or in a six-day creation? No.

God *could have* created the world in six days if he wanted, as "literalists" believe.

However, literal interpretations should not contradict reason or scientific fact, nor should literalists let their belief prevent an honest conversation with non-believers. In a conversation with an unbeliever, I should place the possibility of bringing them to faith (and to salvation) far above my demand that they adhere to a literal interpretation of something that, at this point in their walk of faith,

they find difficult to accept. I'd rather remember what
Jesus said concerning the sabbath: "The Sabbath was
made for man, not man for the Sabbath" (Mk 2:27
NKJV). Likewise, God did not create man to serve a
literal interpretation of the Bible; God inspired biblical
writers to create a book meant to serve man.

The Bible explains how the world began in terms
of events that happened within six "days." The steps
described on each of these "days" correspond with current scientific explanations (for example, plants came
first, then animals, then human beings). But the Genesis
narrative does not seek to lay out a scientific explanation,
but to explain the relationship between God and the
created world, including living things—plants, animals,
and human beings. The story provides an account of
the "Fall" from God's grace, beginning with the original
pair but spreading wider and wider through successive
generations. These "first things" should be understood
literally and figuratively, as appropriate.

An Evangelical turned orthodox Catholic radio
preacher, Hank Hanegraaff, once claimed that the story
of creation in Genesis is do or die for Christianity. He, as
well as other Evangelical ministers I've listened to, maintained that if the Bible's account of the six-day Creation
and the story of Adam and Eve is false, or if evolution
is proven true, then Christianity itself must be false.
Another radio evangelist, Dr. James Kennedy, discounted
a study in which evolutionists argued their point of view,
stating categorically that evolution is wrong because it
differs from his literal interpretation of Genesis 1 to 3.
The major concern, he said, is that the evolutionists

"know if they can prove any part of evolution, then they prove the Bible wrong, and with it all of Christianity wrong."

Such assertions, quite frankly, are wrong—and dangerous. They create a false dichotomy between faith and reason. And they place us and our children at risk. The Bible is a theological document showing the pathway to faith and salvation, a pathway to entering the life of God through the Second Person of the Trinity, Jesus. The Bible is not intended to be more than that. Making this distinction clear is especially important in a world where the "scientific" is considered true, and the "unscientific" false. Many alienate their brothers and sisters from Christ by demanding belief that the world was created only a few thousand years ago. But the truth of Christianity does not depend upon the story of creation, but on the life of a real human being, Jesus Christ.

We must also how such literalist beliefs in these areas of the scriptures place our children in untenable positions. They are being taught they must choose between belief in God and belief in scientific truth. We box them into a corner where they cannot witness to their faith. They are told that if even one item in the Bible (as interpreted in one specific, literal, way) appears false, then Christianity is false and God doesn't exist. Christians who accept this thinking force themselves into defensive, even silly, positions. They retreat in the face of aggressively atheistic evolutionary scientists. Scripture does not exist to promote an understanding of science, politics, or many other secular issues. Although such issues are hugely important to those who seek to live a

Christian life, they are not the reasons Jesus came into the world, nor the reason the Bible was written.

In fact, not only do I believe Dr. Kennedy's statement to be wrong, but it turns the argument upside down. We do not have to prove every statement in the Bible is literally true; Christians are not on the defensive. No, in terms of issues such as evolution, it is the atheist who is on the defensive. For if there is a single instance where science cannot explain the development of the world without an outside force ('God'), then atheism is disproved.

Especially in those parts of the Bible regarding the very beginning and the very end, many assertions will always remain un-provable and stand only as a matter of faith. The correspondence between every word of scripture and scientific explanations does not need to be demonstrated. Faith gets frittered away upon trivialities. We, especially our children, need to understand scripture for what it truly is, respecting those who hold with inflexible interpretations of the Bible but not entering unnecessary and fruitless arguments.[7] Children need to learn how their faith and scripture relate to science as well

---

7. As an engineer, I am dismayed at how people of faith give in to non-believers' false claims that science stands in the way of Christianity. In terms of the "first thigs," too many assume that the twin ideas of the Big Bang and evolution are against the faith. At one point, many scientists and philosophers attempted to disprove God by insisting on an eternal universe with no beginning. Scripture and Christian theology, however, demand the belief that time itself had a beginning when God created the cosmos. That, essentially, is the theme of the theories behind the Big Bang. Second, Christians teach clearly that God is still active in the world. Why should we be surprised that God would change his creation from time to time? That reality can be read into the evolutionary theory, as long as we do not take God out of the equation.

as to other areas of human knowledge like psychology and philosophy. They also need to learn how to dialogue with those who do not accept the truth of the Bible, or who challenge their faith by calling attention to what they believe are tiny inconsistencies in biblical narratives.

The End

In fifty years as a Catholic, I have heard few discussions about the "end times." The Council of Rome (382) and other such conferences confirmed the Book of Revelation to be part of the inspired canon. At every Mass, Catholics sing or recite certain phrases from this final book of the Bible (e.g., "Holy, holy, holy ... "). The lectionary includes several readings from it. Unlike the Evangelical communities I have been part of, however, there is little emphasis on the end times.

Does this mean Revelation is unimportant or un-inspired?

On the contrary, it reassures me that such a symbolic and perhaps confusing book is included in the canon. Just as the difficult sayings from Paul, and, more importantly, from Jesus himself are both a challenge and a comfort. The Bible has not been scrubbed clean of controversy or confusion. Our faith does not rest upon our total understanding of God, who remains eternal and all-powerful, or about the truths behind our own existence.

Christ warned, "It is not for you to know the times or periods that the Father has set by his own authority" (Acts 1:70), so Catholics do not rush into Revelation.

When Jesus told his listeners, "When you hear of wars and rumors of wars, do not be alarmed; this must take place, but the end is still to come. For nation will rise against nation, and kingdom against kingdom; there will be earthquakes in various places; there will be famines.... Beware, keep alert; for you do not know when the time will come" (Mk 13: 7, 33), he wasn't giving pointers concerning what to do at the end of time. No, his words meant something more along these lines: "When these *types* of things happen in the future, do not be confused or afraid. These catastrophes do not necessarily mean I am about to come—for only the Father knows the timing of that event. But when these things do happen don't ever, *ever*, fear that I and the Father have lost control."

The Catholic Church is ancient and has spread over nearly all the world. The Church has witnessed thousands of wars and natural disasters during which it must have seemed as if the end had come. Yet the end *did not come*; the Church therefore recognizes the danger in predicting the second coming and the end of this age. For some, the End indeed has come catastrophically—even today someone will be hit by a bus or gunned down in a gang war or tossed about by a tornado. For others, the end comes quietly in bed. In those circumstances, each person experiences a kind of personal Armageddon—a personal revelation concerning the truth of God and our eternal existence. Jesus' call that we always be prepared applies to each of these people, to every human being who has ever lived. We always need to be always ready. And in times of upheaval never doubt God.

Every Evangelical circle in which I have spent time, be it in a church or through a radio/Internet ministry, places great emphasis on the End Times (in theological terms, "eschatology"). Perhaps it is natural for us to think that we are living during the most decisive of times. Perhaps we see the threats to our well-being as the direst in history, hoping they are important enough that God pays special attention to our needs. This is not to say we should ignore Revelation. We should read that book with the same level of detail and respect as the rest of the Bible. But I have seen that the outcome on my children—perhaps on all children—can be especially damaging if eschatology is not handled correctly.

Sermons on this issue can leave children nervous or fearful, for they don't understand the nuances of the arguments. A sermon on how we may all live through a period of tribulation because the end is at hand needs to convey that this is taught to *steady* their faith. A sermon at a recent Evangelical service explained that the Second Coming must now be very close at hand. The pastor said that in the Middle East many Muslims are coming to Christ, serious problems are plaguing that part of the world, and we are beset by many, many other devilish and strange events—from natural disasters to the Chicago Cubs winning the World Series (and don't make me mention the Red Sox). But similar warnings were given to other Christians in other times—in the Middle Ages, when a third of all Europeans were killed by the plagues, or in our grandparents' lifetimes, when over sixty million souls perished in Nazi, Stalinist, and Maoist wars and persecutions.

At best, warnings that focus on imminent end times create needless anxiety and fear. At worst, such warnings damage the livelihood of people like the followers of Harold Camping, who in 2011 mis-predicted (again) the end of the world. Worse than his followers losing money and having their lives uprooted by his false predication is the fact that every failed prophesy concerning the end of the world causes sincere believers to question their Christian faith and leads those outside the faith to distrust or disparage it.

Again and Again

Basing faith on a literal and personal interpretation of the Bible leads to disregard for the "orthodoxy" established over the long history of the Christian church. Believing anyone can read the Bible alone and the Holy Spirit will provide the *universal* truths behind what is read eliminates the need to respect or learn from the past. Christians who ignore their past leave themselves open to theological and practical errors.

I witnessed this in a recent Evangelical radio sermon. The preacher discussed several heresies in the early Church, heresies that Catholics as well as most Evangelicals have opposed. Many of them concerned the nature of Christ: Was he not man? Was he not God? Was he eternal God, or something created by God? Was he, although humanly Jesus, only a spirit-God who for a while "took" on a human body? And so on. The pastor's explanation of both the heretical and the orthodox position (and how we as a church obtained that orthodox position) all made sense.

He strayed, however, claiming that these heresies (he called them "questions") came about when the early churches attempted to interpret the Bible. Trying to make sense of what was written, those Christians, he said, came up with all sorts of questions, questions that eventually rose to such a level they required a unified answer through the church councils.

There is some truth in this position, for down through the ages adherents and opponents of many heresies have supported their positions by citing scripture. And it does take the Church, guided by the Spirit, to authorize what is considered orthodox.

Something this pastor said, however, struck me as wrong. His error illustrates the well-intentioned yet mistaken notion some Evangelicals hold concerning the Church and scripture. He asserted that in reading the Bible, some local churches realized their doctrines did not correspond to the inspired writings. So, these churches changed their practices to match the Bible; controversies between those who did change and those who didn't led to heresy.

His error lies in placing scripture prior to the Church, making church activity dependent upon adherence to what is written. If the Church were to vanish and a new generation rediscovered the Bible and believed it to be divinely authored, then it would make sense to place the new Church and the Bible in that order. However, Jesus first formed the Church through Peter and the apostles. Some questions emerged very early as the Church grew (i.e. whether to include Gentiles or not; whether to require circumcision or not, etc.). Some of these issues in fact were dealt with and answered when the Church, then barely decades old, held its first council in Jerusalem–before most of the New Testament had been written.

Some, such as the Judaizers, rejected the leaders' decisions. They became, to a degree, "heretical" by subjecting Gentile Christians to the Mosaic Law. But their break with orthodoxy was not a difference in scriptural interpretation, for it would be three hundred years until the writings circulated in the communities would be codified into the New Testament. No one reading St. Paul's warnings in Galatians against this "false gospel" of the Judaizers considered his letter to be "scripture" when they received it. No, the infant church rejected the Judaizers' views as "heretical" because they opposed what the Church, upon the testimony of Peter and the apostles, already accepted and determined at the Council of Jerusalem.

It was not until the decades following Pentecost, when the apostles had spread out to preach the Word to the nations and establish communities beyond Jerusalem, that Paul wrote the letters that today are included in the New Testament. Most of what the gospel authors wrote were not new ideas inspired by the Holy Spirit. Their writings reflected the tradition of the young apostolic Church and the direct memories of what Christ taught and how he lived, as well as the general beliefs and practices being lived out in the early Christian communities. Luke begins his Gospel like this:

> *Many* have *undertaken* to draw up an account
> of the things that have been fulfilled among
> us, just as they were *handed down* to us by
> those who from the first were *eyewitnesses*

and servants of the word. With this in mind, since I myself have carefully investigated everything from the beginning, I too decided to write an orderly account for you. (Lk 1:1-3, NIV, italics added)

How did fourth century church leaders determine what to *accept* as canonical and what to *reject*? They tried to identify the true authorship of each prospective book *and* determine if a particular text reflected the generally accepted life and teachings of the churches already in place. For example, followers of Arius believed Jesus was not truly God. From the time of Christ to the approval of the biblical canon, the principal apostolic churches taught that Jesus was truly God, one with the Father and the Trinity. Some writings used by various local Christian churches up to the time of Arius in fourth century could be interpreted as supporting the central tenets of Arianism, as could some words and phrases in the gener ally accepted writings of the faith, including some that have been incorporated into our current New Testament.

When the Arian heresy came to a head around the time of Council at Nicaea, however, the books that the Church determined to be "divinely inspired" supported the belief that Jesus was God, or at the very least they did not demand the Arian view. After long debate, the Nicene Creed included the definition of Christ as true God-Man (as opposed to the Man-Pretending-to-be-God, or demi-God) based upon the tradition of the Church, the writings of the fathers of the church, and the beliefs generally held within Christianity.

Even recently, in a radio broadcast from Grace
Bible Church in Illinois, Pastor Philippi taught that the
Gospel of John was written to the Jews to convey a proper
understanding of Jesus as the Messiah. But, said the pastor, in writing to the Gentiles Paul sought to convey a
proper understanding of *how* we are saved—that Christ
died as our replacement on the cross. What John sought
to convey to the Jewish community is therefore not *our*
"good news." The pastor maintained that for us living in
the "but now" (a phrase taken from a Paul's Letter to the
Ephesians), we only need follow what Paul wrote, and
not the Gospels or other works like the Letter of James
that he believes were directed only to the Jews.

Pastor Philippi certainly demonstrates a "sola scriptura" approach, but it leads him toward a heresy that the
Church faced 1800 years ago. Like other thinkers who
have strayed from orthodoxy, his argument operates from
human logic, by which theology can be based on a individual's personal interpretation of scripture. But he con-
tradicts the tradition and orthodoxy of the faith, falling
into a heresy that dates to the second century. Marcion
of Sinope taught that Christian faith rested only upon
ten letters from Paul, the Letter to the Hebrews and a
version of the Gospel of Luke (which he believed Paul
also wrote). If we ignore those who came before us and
assume the Holy Spirit is guiding us and us alone, it is
likely that we will fall again and again away from the true
Christian faith.

Final Authority

The late R.C. Sproul, rooted in a Calvinistic "Reformed" approach to scripture, also professed sola scriptura, using his interpretation of the Bible to determine proper doctrine or church practice. In a radio sermon concerning the development and meaning of the Nicene Creed, Sproul seemed to acknowledge the Catholic point of view that revelation and authority come through scripture together with the tradition of the Church. The Church, founded by Jesus Christ, had the authority to discern the canon of the Bible. To do this, the Church draws upon its experience—its tradition—together with the biblical record. But Dr. Sproul then pursued a long and logically tortuous path to show that this was not true. He maintained that the Evangelical position of scripture alone is the only correct Christian outlook.

His argument began in 1563 with the Council of Trent. Facing a decades-old Reformation, the Catholic Church officially reiterated its position that both scripture and tradition determine Christian "truth." Sproul emphasized a couple of notes from certain sessions of the council that showed two priests protesting the proposed language of its published "canons," preferring wording that indicated the supremacy of scripture over tradition. Dr. Sproul then dismissed the final wording accepted by the council which used the Latin word "et" ("and") to state how truth has been revealed through scripture *and* tradition, focusing instead on the two priests' preference for what he considered to be more "Protestant" language. In other words, he argued that the Holy Spirit properly guided these two priests, but not the whole of the Church.

Sproul then turned his attention twelve hundred years earlier, to the Council of Nicaea in 325. It makes sense to do so, for it was at Nicaea and other Councils and synods during that era where the Church codified its Trinitarian beliefs, as articulated in the Nicene Creed, and began to establish the New Testament canon. The "scriptura" of sola scriptura is based upon these fourth century decisions. Again, Dr. Sproul examined the language used at the time. In this case, he focused upon a word used by these councils, "received." The word "received," as in "we *receive* these books as the inspired Word of God," suggested to him that the Church was not actually "approving" these books from a position of authority, but that these books were so obviously God's inerrant truth the bishops simply *received* them as true and then accepted God's requirement to follow them. They had no choice. In other words, the Church received—accepted—what God had already provided. The scriptures therefore had authority in and of themselves; the Church never possessed authority over them.

I'm willing to accept Sproul's contention that the word "received" employed by these Councils was used in the same sense we would use it today. It is obvious, however, that Jesus did not write the books of the New Testament with his own finger. During those first centuries of the Church, over a hundred different books had been used by one or another of the early churches to teach Christians their faith. In the fourth and fifth centuries, again as a matter of historical fact, the Church (in meetings attended by Augustine and others) chose from those writings only the ones they were convinced to have been inspired by the Holy Spirit. Through the wisdom of that same Holy Spirit and through the power granted them by Christ as successors to the apostles, the bishops chose some of those early books and rejected others. Those they chose, again as attested by church history, corresponded to orthodox Christian doctrine at the time. In this way, the Church had authority to choose the books of the New Testament and exercised that authority to codify the Bible we use today.

After these decisions, church leaders saw no conflicts between the newly "canonized" scripture and the tradition of the existing Christian communities. Nothing in any of the accepted books of scripture required changes in doctrine or practices in order to correspond with the newly approved testament. No changes to the hierarchical structure of the Church, no changes to the sacraments, no changes to the proper use of scripture and tradition. In terms of receiving heretics back into the faith, church leaders did not specifically point to any single interpretation of scripture but Canon VIII, in a straightforward requirement stated, "that they will observe and follow the dogmas of the Catholic and Apostolic Church."

However, in approving the canon (defined as such for the next thousand years), the councils did not pore over Acts or Romans or James, approving or disapproving each individual word or phrase. They did "accept" or "receive" in full each book in what we now know as the New Testament. But the council fathers did not "receive" *everything* they had at their disposal then written about Christ. Through the Church's understanding and authority, the council fathers accepted some books wholly and rejected other books wholly. It is significant and reassuring that in the texts they accepted and received they left even some sayings from Christ we still puzzle over.

Although a canon is established, some churches continue to dispute what parts of scripture to emphasize. When I first began attending Evangelical services I found a strong priority given to the writings of Paul, and lesser attention to the story of Christ as told in the gospels. Other Evangelical leaders, including R.C. Sproul, have criticized this tendency, warning against placing Paul against Christ, or against Matthew, or against Luke. Sproul advised against such opposition because we have nothing written by Christ himself. What we know about Jesus comes from the four Gospels; what Paul wrote can only correspond to the words of God about the Word of God.

The critical issue, however, is the role that scripture plays in the Church as a whole. This issue is obviously quite beyond the scope of this book, so I will only relay what I think summarizes the issue best, and this not from a Catholic but from a Protestant, Bishop Leslie Newbigin, in his book, *The Household of God*:

> At the heart and centre of the earthly min-
> istry of the incarnate Christ was the choos-
> ing, training and sending forth of a band of
> apostles. If His purpose had been to provide
> for all succeeding generations of mankind a
> revelation of God which could be embodied
> in a series of verbal statements of absolute
> inerrancy, or an infallible code of conduct,

He could have left a written deposit. But it is precisely what he did not do.... At the very end He told them that He had much more yet to tell them. If divine revelation means a complete communication of the whole counsel of God to me, then we have it on His own authority that He did not give it.[8]

We know more about Christ than what is written in the Gospels. For example, what did Luke mean when he wrote, "I myself have carefully investigated everything from the beginning"? What evidence did he investigate? Certainly, he discovered the teachings, life, death, and resurrection of Christ as remembered by those who lived with Jesus and for decades formed a church which had spread the faith. Luke found the Lord not in the Old Testament or within the pages of what is now in the rest of the New Testament. He, as with Paul who after his experience on the road to Damascus was instructed by those already in the Church, came to know Christ through his bride, the Church, which has continued to speak the truth to us for the past two thousand years.

It is through this Church, then, that we receive what is most important to us—a clear understanding of the gospel, the Good News that we can experience the kingdom of God in this life and in the next. That we, sinners all, have both a Savior and a Lord—Jesus the Christ.

---

8. Leslie Newbigin, *The Household of God* (London: SCM Press, 1953), 61.

Chapter 4

The Good News

"Do not be afraid."
          —Jesus Christ (Mt 28:10)
"Be not afraid"
          —St. John Paul II (April 2, 2006)

On December 26, 2010, Chris Wallace of Fox News Sunday interviewed Cardinal Donald Wuerl of Washington DC. Wallace asked, "In this special season, what message do you have for Christians and non-Christians alike?"

The cardinal answered,

Christmas is a time when we all can look with hope to the future. That's part of the message of Christmas. There is the best in each one of us. And we're all capable of bringing out the best. And to do that together with one another, in a very pluralistic society, says that we can look to the future with hope, because if we respect and love one another, there is nothing we can't accomplish.

In this book, I strive to bring together Catholics and non-Catholic Christians from my personal experiences in both faith communities. This requires a clear explanation of those things in my Catholic faith and practice that are problematic for other Christians and stand in the way of proclaiming a common gospel. Therefore, perhaps, my experience in Evangelical churches has sensitized me more than I would have been as a Catholic prior to my exposure to non-Catholics. Certainly, the Cardinal in this interview was exercising extreme caution as Wallace asked him to address a national audience of "Christians and non-Christians alike."

Still, I regretted the Cardinal's answer. At Christmas especially, how can a Christian leader say nothing about Christ? How can we proclaim hope in our earthly potential but not even mention our true Hope in a heavenly future? As C.S. Lewis said, "It is since Christians have largely ceased to think of the other world that they have become so ineffective in this."[9] Just as importantly, how can non-Catholics witness the truth in the Catholic faith, or at the very least see us as Christian, if we are not willing to publicly announce our faith in Christ?

This is not to attack Cardinal Wuerl or his faith, which I assume is strong and sincere, but only this particular answer. It did not distinguish Christianity, specifically Catholic Christianity, from any other purveyors of practical wisdom that saturate our culture. According to such wisdom, people are free to choose the philosophy they think more comfortable or more exciting or most fitting. The Cardinal's answer did not call attention to Jesus' unique message, even at Christmas. Instead, he

---

9. C.S. Lewis, *Mere Christianity* (New York: Harper One, 1980), 134.

offered an anodyne statement about looking "with hope to the future," "the best in each one of us," "respect and love one another," "nothing we can't accomplish."

Such an attitude and approach runs deep—and often unnoticed—within Catholic universities, hospitals, and other institutions. Go to this Catholic college, the brochures emphasize, not because Catholicism offers a key to eternal life, but because the school's philosophy and methods provide a more well-rounded education useful in making you a better person *in this life*. Following an anonymous path of "respect and love" does not assure a better life here or in the next world; it leads to the stagnation of faith or even to its death. Death for our faith, death for our souls.

Catholics could profit from the approach taken by our Evangelical brothers and sisters. *Do not be afraid* to challenge people out of a desire to avoid offense. Do not offend on purpose, of course, but as Kierkegaard emphasized in *Practice in Christianity*, Jesus himself *came to offend*, and those who were and are saved are those *who are not offended* by his message of being the God-man. The message of our sins. The message of our need for a Savior and Lord.

People should choose Catholic schools to equip themselves for *eternal life*. People should come to Christian faith not because it might improve this life but because it will prepare them for *the next life*. People are not drawn to *Christ* because his philosophy is better than that of other gurus and teachers but because he is the Way, the Truth and the Life. The forgiveness of sins and the inheritance of eternal life with God—this is the

Good News, the greatest of all news, even if we discover that believing in Christ can upend our lives on Earth. Catholics, all billion plus of them, are called to engage in a new evangelization that brings people to the truth. Jesus said, "Strive first for the kingdom of God and his righteousness, and all these things will be given to you as well" (Mt 6:33). The true Good News of everlasting life is priceless; in the end, nothing else has lasting value.

To achieve ecumenical respect for each other and move toward effective unity, we need to be bold about what unifies us. Some Catholics leave the Church to worship within Evangelical communities because they find better music, better or more congenial companionship with other laypeople, or because of a different emphasis on the Bible. But most Catholics I know who have become Evangelicals do so because what Catholicism stands for has come to seem vague and lifeless, whereas their new Evangelical church seems to have a clearer purpose, passionate and bold: focus and persuade first, last and always, concerning our salvation through Christ and the eternity he offers. Do not be afraid. Do not tire. All else in our world will improve only after we embrace the Life of Christ, and without this Life, nothing will improve forever.

We can learn here from Evangelicals' enthusiasm and methods. They are passionate and bold in their proclamation of the faith and their efforts to draw people to Christ. Even though Catholics and Evangelicals may need to de-emphasize or reconsider certain practices for the sake of unity, Christian unity never benefits from silence regarding our faith in the Lord.

Some religious leaders, whether Catholic or from another Christian church, seem to avoid giving offense, and there is a time and wisdom for this. But churches offer one thing no one else can, one thing down through the centuries to which people have returned while lesser things come and go.

Beyond any philosophy only one Truth endures: Jesus Christ.

Who (not What) Is the Good News?

My children and I have experienced two Christian faith communities in depth. They may grow up to be more understanding and tolerant due to this exposure, but I also worry they may accept new philosophies with less discerning eyes. I have found it important these past few years to think deeply about the fundamental points of Christian theology. Having the benefit (and sometimes confusion) of drawing from two different traditions, phrases, terminology, and emphases, I have tried to determine the truly Christian beliefs we share. To understand the Good News and our eternal life with God we must begin (and end) with Jesus.

Analogies—only representations of an actual thing—are always imperfect. Even a thousand words cannot convey the mental picture created by a good analogy. This is one reason why Christ taught in parables. The powerful, vivid mental images in these stories have remained within the Church for 2000 years and speak to people of every language and culture.

How can the Good News be described adequately? Who is this Jesus in relation to us?

Christ is both God and man, a being like us yet our ultimate moral teacher, Savior, and Lord. As a fellow human being, Jesus demonstrates how to subordinate our pride to the Father's will. Only a *perfect man* could approach the level of righteousness necessary to demonstrate how we are to live a properly humble life. A sinful man humbling himself before God is just being realistic. A perfect, all-powerful Man humbling himself before the Father is the only truly effective example for human beings in terms of how we are to consider our own relationship with our Creator.

Yet even a *perfect man* could experience suffering that exceeds the capacity of his human will. Were Christ simply a man, even a perfect man, his unbearable torture could have made him rebel against the Father. But Jesus *chose* to remain on the cross. As God, he had the power to come down; instead, through his final moment of perfect submission he reversed Adam's prideful rebellion. Through this choice he achieved our salvation and opened a relationship with "Abba," our Father.

In *The Everlasting Man*, G.K. Chesterton says:

> No sufferings of the sons of men, or even the servants of God, strike the same note as the notion of the master suffering instead of his servants. No mysterious monarch, hidden in his starry pavilion at the base of the cosmic campaign, is in the least like that celestial chivalry of the Captain who carries his five wounds to the front of battle.

Nothing short of the extreme and strong and startling doctrine of the divinity of Christ will give that particular effect that can truly stir the popular sense like a trumpet … as the idea of the king himself serving in the ranks like a common soldier. [10]

But the Good News goes even further than this. No other faith comes close to that of a Father willing to give up his Son in sacrifice to save others, especially the unworthy. Yet even this does not go deep enough to express what the Good News means.

"Eli, eli lama sabachthani," Christ groaned on the cross. "My God, my God, why have you forsaken me?" At that final moment, the Son was willing to empty himself of who he is—eternal God—to experience full and complete abandonment by the Father, to experience fully our human frailty and weakness. In this very moment on the cross, he presents the perfect example of fulfilled humanity, our selves emptied before the holy God.

But that event also contains a further drama which shook the world. Can we not imagine God the Father echoing his Son in that very moment—"Hyios, hyios …"? *"My Son, my Son, why have you forsaken me?"* While the Father cannot "feel" as humans do, it has helped me to appreciate the depth of his love to consider that as "Father" he was pleased with his Son's sacrifice. For the Son loved us so much that he was willing to allow his

---

10. G.K. Chesterton, *The Everlasting Man* (San Francisco: Ignatius Press, 1993), 242.

eternal relationship with the Father to be shattered for those precious moments.

Perhaps we might consider this as the separation between a human parent and a child who matures and leaves the family. How, in this case, the child so loved others that he was willing to break his family bond in other to help those in desperate need, no matter the cost to his father. And the Father also shows love and tender mercy for us, placing aside his bond with his Son for our good. He was not a Father who "punished" his Son, but a Father who with his Son loved us perfectly through his Son's sacrifice. A God who allowed himself, in a way, to be ripped in two, to feel through Jesus' death the unfathomable loss of self and the communion with his own Son. That love of the Father for us, deeper than any human can imagine, is truly the Good News.

A Personal Relationship

Evangelicals often justify division from Catholics primarily over the effect of "faith" versus "works" in salvation. A second aspect of this issue is summarized in what they consider to be a "personal relationship" with Jesus. They claim Catholics believe salvation is earned through "works," which therefore do not require friendship with or reliance upon Christ. Even the completely godless can do good works for the needy out of a sense of simple duty or compassion. But without Christ, such works cannot bring the forgiveness needed for an eternal relationship with God.

On the other hand, if you believe you can achieve eternal life only through faith in Christ, then you must have a relationship with him. Of course, you can accept that Jesus died for us without liking him, much less loving him. Nevertheless, the Evangelical perspective construes this relationship between ourselves and Christ as being between best friends, feeling an intellectual and emotional response to what Christ has done for us. Of course, all Christians should seek a personal relationship with Jesus. It is the most effective and fulfilling way of maintaining faith. When our emotions dry up, our faith can depend more upon intellectual steadiness; when we experience doubt and exhaustion, faith often requires blind passion.

Arguing that one group of Christians has a personal relationship with Jesus but another group does not demonstrates enormous pride. It takes effort and almost divine insight to determine if one person has the "proper" personal relationship with another person, much less with Christ. It is the height of ego to believe only those like ourselves know how to respond to our Lord. For thirty years, I read at least one chapter of the Bible every night (and three on Sundays). As work, parenthood, and everything else God brought my way reduced my available time (and the ability to keep my eyes open late at night), my reading of scripture became inconsistent. Now, I often replace my nightly time in the Word with listening to radio and on-line sermons while driving, reading other religious books, and researching for my own writing. Some may see my lack of direct biblical study reflecting a lack of personal relationship with Jesus.

Yet during these past years of struggle, my faith and daily response to God's call has grown ever stronger. My work often causes over-the-top frustration and worry and even panic. An outsider might consider this an undue focus on *things* and a lack of faith in Christ. Yet those moments of pain and trouble have often brought me closer to Jesus than did times of happiness, gratitude and plenty.

No one has the right to judge someone else's personal relationship with Jesus. God himself knows how we can best keep close to him. We should read the Bible, attend church services, receive the Eucharist, spend time on our knees in prayer. But Christians must take great care before criticizing someone because we think they are following the *wrong* path to Jesus. We may think that our faith adheres more closely to the guidance of Jesus and his apostles, but we must also realize that the Holy Spirit is working in each of us. Catholics ought not judge Evangelicals because their relationship with Jesus does not include the Eucharist, and Evangelicals ought not criticize Catholics for lacking a relationship with Christ because they don't raise their hands in exuberant song and worship.

A teenager weeping during a Christian youth group song or an elderly nun on her knees in adoration before the body and blood of Christ are both experiencing a powerful "personal" relationship with the same Lord. The regularities of the Mass can lead to the perception that Catholics are simply "going through the motions." Evangelicals, who say we need to *feel* God's presence, to be "in love" with him, to sing loudly during weekly services and get charged up by the preaching, can appear to be substituting an emotional, feel-good high for a personal and thoughtful relationship with the Lord. Both styles can be abused and lead us from God, and both styles have strengths that can build our friendship and trust in our Lord.

In sixth grade, I read that God would grant me anything I asked for through Christ, so I prayed every hour at school that a certain girl would ask me out (since I was far too shy to ask her). Childish, no doubt. Yet over and over throughout the day it brought me before the Lord. On Sundays my parents sometimes went to an early Mass, but I would still walk "religiously" the three or more miles to church by myself when I could have been outside playing with my friends. A young boy who at that point in his life knew only the Catholic faith, I nonetheless had a very close relationship with God. In high school, one night a week I attended an inter-denominational Christian youth group with a few Evangelical friends. Many of my peers fell into drinking and other youthful transgressions, but I doodled the cross on my notebooks and stayed away from alcohol and drugs. In college, despite the lure of major college athletics and the complete freedom of dorm life, I continued to go to weekly Mass and to read the Bible, my daily walk with the Lord. I recollect how every Mass nearly brought me to tears as I thought about how Jesus suffered and died for me, and how far I was from his ideal "me."

Perhaps I have indeed been over-exposed to Evangelical thought. I longed for the cardinal's Christmas message to encourage us concerning where we should focus our desire—upon improving the world, to be sure, but first and foremost on our personal, communal and eternal relationship with Christ and his Church. Catholics indeed must speak more openly about our faith, see moments within each day where we can come closer to Jesus. Evangelicals, on the other hand, need to acknowledge that a personal relationship with Jesus may not always be stimulating, feel-good, and exciting.

What Was That Church?

Over the course of two millennia, in every culture and circumstance, faith in Christ has been born, has grown, has been beaten down only to rise again stronger.

This is the genius of Christ.

And yet to speak of God incarnate as having "genius" is not enough. Applying a word like genius to Christ has the effect of de-divinizing him, depicting him as if he was not Man, but merely a great man, and certainly not God. It suggests we should admire Jesus for his intelligence and wisdom when we ought to worship the God-man who by his very being defines intelligence and wisdom.

How did the church founders, under the guidance of the Holy Spirit, bring the Good News to the world? Beginning with the day of Pentecost in Jerusalem, the apostles established the Church, which grew rapidly throughout the Middle East and then the entire Roman world. The men who lived with Christ and witnessed his resurrection told and retold the stories of his life and teaching, a need that Luke expresses clearly at the beginning of his Gospel:

> Since many have undertaken to set down an orderly account of the events that have been fulfilled among us, just as they were handed on to us by those who from the beginning were eyewitnesses and servants of the word, I too decided, after investigating everything carefully from the very first, to write an orderly account ... so that you may know the truth concerning the things about which you have been instructed. (Lk 1:1-2)

The accounts written between thirty and seventy years after Christ's ascension focused on the issues most important to the writers and the members of the infant Church. One of the first to follow Jesus was Peter. In his Gospel and in the Book of Acts, St. Luke (Paul's long-time companion) describes Peter as the leader of the Church. Peter became the first Bishop of Rome. Catholics claim him as the first pope, the vicar (representative or deputy) of Christ.

Within that early apostolic Church also lived James, the first bishop in Jerusalem after Peter departed for Rome; Nicolas the Deacon led the first "Christians" in Antioch; and St. Mark the Evangelist led the Church in the fourth chief Roman city, Alexandria. Then came Paul, who went to Peter and the others in that first council to obtain approval and blessing and direction for his mission to the Gentiles. Next came the first waves of martyrdom and whirlwind growth in the faith across the Roman world. Within decades of Christ's sacrifice, the form and worship of the earliest churches is documented, including descriptions of the sacraments, discussions about the theological differences among the earliest church fathers, and the first inklings of what would later become the great heresies of the early faith. These heresies caused the debates and discussions which led to the beliefs codified in the Nicene Creed and used to define Christians for the next 1700 years

As G.K. Chesterton said in *Everlasting Man:*

Out of this (Mediterranean) culture arose the Christian religion and the Catholic Church; and everything in the story suggests that it was felt to be something new and strange. Those who have tried to suggest that it evolved out of something much milder or more ordinary have found that in this case their evolutionary method is very difficult to apply.... The tree (of the Church) appears very rapidly full-grown; and the tree is something totally different ... that very early in its history this thing became visible to the civilization of antiquity; and that already the Church appeared as a Church; with everything that is implied in a Church and much that is disliked in a Church. It was certainly not in the least like a merely ethical and idealistic movement.... It has a doctrine; it had a discipline; it had sacraments; it had degrees of initiation; it admitted people and expelled people; it affirmed one dogma with authority and repudiated another.... If all of these things be the mark of Antichrist, the reign

of Antichrist followed very rapidly upon
Christ. (217)

At its beginning, the Church faced the same human
and functional issues that churches do now. The New
Testament, particularly the Book of Acts, offers accounts
of the earliest followers of Christ who in Jesus had witnessed a living bridge between the human and the divine.
They struggled to make from their own weaknesses
something worthy of Jesus, who they had seen rise from
the dead and ascend into heaven. These early Christians,
who knew Christ personally, still had different opinions
in some areas. But the early Church did not see any reason or justification for division. The first Christians did
not seem to believe they had the authority to leave the
faith of the apostles.

Perhaps this loyalty came from the deep humility
anyone who had been in the presence of the risen Christ
should and would feel. Peter and Paul, two primary
figures in the early Christian communities, displayed
modesty and obedience to the Church. Paul toiled in
obscurity for years before bringing his case concerning
the Gentiles before Peter and the rest of the established
leadership. And Peter, hand-picked by Jesus himself,
humbled himself before Paul's scolding after siding at
one point with the "Judaizers." Peter had such a change
of heart he seems to have relinquished the Jewish culture
that had defined his life. He went to the very center of
the pagan world, Rome, to establish the mother church
and to die as a martyr.

The Church at that time was largely united in doctrine, as Christ had commanded and prayed for. One in

their belief in the Jewish God; one in their belief in the resurrection and the ascension; one in their goal to live and proclaim the Good News.

The early books of Paul and other followers of Jesus reflect this unified faith. Paul, as well as the other New Testament authors, wrote when most of the great apostles were still alive. Peter clearly read Paul's words, for he comments about them directly (2 Pt 3:15). Others, like John, outlived Paul. In fact, John's Gospel was put into written form long after Paul's martyrdom. Surely, if Peter or John or any of the other apostles who lived with and learned directly from Jesus found anything heretical in Paul's writings, they would have objected. Since they knew Christ personally and Paul did not, at least not in the flesh, their opinions would have prevailed. They affirmed the light that had come to Saul of Tarsus, persecutor of the early Christian community; and their unity serves as a model for how Christian churches today ought to work together "so that the world may believe."

The Creed

The Church is more than a building, a congregation, a set of rituals and ceremonies. The Christian Church is defined by a body of beliefs by which its members give themselves to Christ, giving glory to the Father by becoming more like their Savior. So, what fundamental beliefs distinguish and nourish a Christian, even without the walls of a church building, even without the Bible? These beliefs are stated succinctly in the creeds.

Most Evangelicals use the Apostles' Creed, which many believe originated with those who lived with Jesus. But, and this was a great surprise to me, the Apostles' Creed did not originate with the apostles. In fact, it was first documented almost sixty years after the Nicene Creed was formulated.

The Nicene Creed emerged from the Church's understanding of Jesus as stated by his apostles, passed down through generations of the bishops and other leaders of the early churches, and reflected in what would come to be accepted as the scriptural canon. This creed articulated "orthodox" Christianity during an era marked by heretical and false teachings. It recapitulates what Paul shared with the community at Corinth:

> For I handed on to you as of first importance what I in turn had received: that Christ died for our sins in accordance with the scriptures, and that he was buried, and that he was raised on the third day in accordance with the scriptures, and that he appeared to Cephas, then to the twelve. Then he appeared to more than five hundred brothers and sisters at one time, most of whom are still alive. (1 Cor 15: 3-6)

This creed delineates Christian belief concerning the Trinity, explains the Church the Lord left to us, and gives a glimpse into our eternal future. It serves as a unifying statement of the Christian faith, since through this creed Christians developed the foundational Trinitarian view of God, and the concise reasons for Christ's life, ministry, death and resurrection. The creed does not

tell us how we are to live, or how we are to worship, or
what we are to read. Its focus is instead upon God; it is
a humble statement of our shared faith, and it should
stand as the definition of what it means to be Christian.

> I believe in one God, the Father almighty,
> maker of heaven and earth, of all things
> visible and invisible.

> I believe in one Lord, Jesus Christ, the Only
> Begotten Son of God, born of the Father
> before all ages.

> God from God, Light from Light, true
> God from true God, begotten, not made,
> consubstantial with the Father; through him
> all things were made.

> For us men and for our salvation he came
> down from heaven, and by the Holy Spirit
> was incarnate of the Virgin Mary and became
> man.

> For our sake he was crucified under Pontius
> Pilate, he suffered death and was buried, and
> rose again on the third day in accordance
> with the Scriptures.

> He ascended into heaven and is seated at the
> right hand of the Father. He will come again
> in glory to judge the living and the dead and
> his kingdom will have no end.

> I believe in the Holy Spirit, the Lord, the
> giver of life, who proceeds from the Father

and the Son, who with the Father and the Son is adored and glorified, who has spoken through the prophets.

I believe in one, holy, catholic and apostolic Church.

I confess one Baptism for the forgiveness of sins and I look forward to the resurrection of the dead and the life of the world to come.

Who Can Receive the Good News?

Who then can receive the saving truth found in the Creed? The Catholic Church promotes an inclusive view that Jesus came to save the "whole world." While some see the idea of "inclusivity" as universalism, meaning "everything is acceptable," "inclusive" here denotes only the willingness to accept as Christian any who profess faith in Christ, even if they lack full union or even unity with one's own preferred expression of the faith. Inclusiveness does not mean those who do not follow Christ participate in God's family in the same way Christian believers do. However, Catholic teaching does not presume to condemn those who may not explicitly claim faith in Christ, since they are still children of God, who desires their eternal salvation.

The *Catechism of the Catholic Church* states:

All men are bound to seek the truth, especially in what concerns God and his Church, and to embrace it and hold on to it as they

come to know it. This duty derives from
the very dignity of the human person. It
does not contradict a sincere respect for different religions which frequently reflect a
ray of that truth which enlightens all men,
nor the requirement of charity, which urges
Christians to treat with love, prudence and
patience those who are in error or ignorant
with regard to the faith. (2104)

The Catholic Church acknowledges it is not known
who will be saved and who will not. We cannot *tell* God
whom to condemn. We cannot limit God's saving power.
We know God laid out a path to salvation through faith
in Christ but have yet to discover how or if God takes
care of our brothers and sisters who do not know Christ
and his Church.

Jesus told a parable about workers hired late in
the day who earned the same—and fair—wages as those
hired earlier in the day. His point is that we cannot and
should not presume to tell each other (or God) how people should be rewarded, or who is worthy or unworthy of
eternal life through Jesus Christ. Unbelievers should not
be treated as stumbling through life on a hopeless path,
but as somehow being with us on the same path toward
God through Christ. Everyone needs Christ, and we do
our part in evangelization by helping our brothers and
sisters find the truth, not browbeating them as enemies.

The *Catechism* also teaches that "all men are called
to this catholic unity of the People of God" (836). The
Catholic Church acknowledges other religions that search

"for God who is unknown (to them) yet near since he gives life and breath and all things and wants all men to be saved" (843). The Church considers the goodness and truth found in other religions to be "a preparation for the Gospel and given by him who enlightens all men that they may at length have life" (843); and again, "Those who, through no fault of their own, do not know the Gospel of Christ or his Church, but who nevertheless seek God with a sincere heart ... those too *may* achieve eternal salvation" (847). Jesus said, "Whatever you bind on earth will be bound in heaven, and whatever you loose on earth will be loosed in heaven" (Mt 18:18).

True Christians emphasize the "loosing." We are to forgive freely. Unity demands that we apply the Lord's statement to others and to *ourselves*. If we forgive ("loose") others, our own sins will be forgiven (as reflected in the Lord's Prayer). In dealing with those who do not believe, we need first to *forgive* them, to see their lack of faith not as a failure or as rejection of Jesus, but as a reflection of simple ignorance or the pride all human beings share.

Jesus did say "I am the way, and the truth, and the life. No one comes to the Father except through me" (Jn 14:6). Some take that to mean a personal profession of faith in Jesus is the *only* way to salvation. Anyone opposing this view is seen as insulting both the Bible and our Lord. Believing we are saved only if we have faith in Christ and focusing on Jesus' central role in redemption does generate a positive urgency to share the gospel with non-Christians. A gentle, non-condemning approach (similar to how we see St. Paul address the Athenians [Acts 17: 15-34]) better reaches unbelievers who need to be respected and brought slowly to faith.

Does Christ then save good people of every nation and faith, even if they may not believe in him? And does this mean we, regardless of our "religion," are part of God's grand design? Are we truly brothers and sisters at a deeper level than we now acknowledge? Are we all, to some degree, capable of receiving and benefiting from the Good News and Christ's Church?

The answer, thankfully, is "Yes."

Christ is the only way to Life. We need Jesus to achieve union with God and salvation. God is all-powerful and could save us without our having an explicit Christian faith. Nevertheless, God wants us to have something to do with our salvation. Christ clearly call us to "knock" and to "seek" and to "believe." We can and should thank God for even the slightest desire we find within us to do these things, but we do *do* something. And if there is something for us to *do*, then there must be a right and effective thing for us to do, and many incorrect and ineffective things we could do that we shouldn't. No one claims we should seek false unity by denying our responsibility to discover and follow the correct ways. It is right, however, to seek Christ, knock on the Holy Spirit's door, and believe in the Triune God.

"Doing" or "believing" anything else may not lead us to God. Jesus opened the path to heaven, without our help or prior belief, and we honor him and his sovereignty by believing that he can save all people, however he chooses. We are called, as Evangelicals emphasize, to see each Christian as a soul Christ has found and brought to everlasting life. But, we cannot deny anyone hope or disregard their honest attempts to heed God's small voice and to live the best lives they can under their own circumstances. We ought not alienate anyone or condemn them as being without hope due to their struggles in accepting the fullness of Christian truth.

The Evangelicals I have lived with downplay Jesus' physical nature in various areas—not believing, for example, that Christ is physically present in the Eucharist, or removing physical representations of Christ in churches. Nevertheless, at the same time they also demand that "belief in Jesus" and salvation through him alone requires belief in a specific physical person who lived two thousand years ago in Palestine. I believe in this physical Jesus, the historic flesh-and-blood Christ. It is the one path we know for sure will lead us toward salvation. Focusing on Jesus in this human way, however, and restricting God's power to include among the saved more than those who know of and believe in this physical "man," can distract from the fact that Jesus is also one Person in the triune God. Doing so over-emphasizes his humanity and diminishes his divinity. In other words, since Jesus is God, anyone who believes he or she is a sinner and asks God for forgiveness is asking this of Jesus. Acknowledging that Jesus is more than his physical reality does not diminish the fullness of the Christian faith, or his work while physically alive, or the need to know and believe in the "real" Jesus. It expands the role and work of Christ. This insight has helped me reconcile my belief in a merciful God when considering those who never have heard of the historic Jesus. For those who have heard, much is required, including believing in Christ and obeying him. But, somehow, God's plan for those who have not heard is also both "fair" and true to who Christ is.

It honors Christ to understand of him as God and the object of worship for all believers, not just Christians. Christ has the power to save even those who have never seen or heard of him. For example, the physical "me" can only save the physical "you," by physically pushing you out of the way of the speeding train. You can only be helped by me if we encounter each other and make physical contact. But Christ ... God ... might he not also have the power to save those who have never seen or heard of him? We honor him by accepting his sovereign power to help his beloved brothers and sisters in ways ordinary humans cannot.

Us Against the World

Some Evangelicals hold a narrow view regarding who is part of God's family and who isn't. This is a stumbling block for ecumenism, the search for Christian unity. It is impossible to develop such unity if one group of Christians does not consider the other to be Christian at all. This issue took on great importance for me when it touched directly upon my children's faith.

Evangelical churches are highly focused upon missions. In their missionary spirit—the emphasis upon the laity's personal role in evangelizing the world—Evangelical churches surpass my Catholic experience. Their zeal for spreading the word, their focus on doing so through ordinary people instead of mainly through the clergy, is something Catholic laypeople can and should imitate. Missionary families, including those with children, can sometimes open pathways for communicating the gospel with more impact and success than the celibate clergy and religious. Those of us who haven't followed the missionary path are inspired by photos and videos of people putting their lives on pause to reach new souls for Christ. It is humbling to witness their sacrifices, their hardships, their amazing ability to put aside careers, say goodbye to friends and family, and move half-way around the world.

It is appropriate to celebrate such activities before the whole church family. One missionary, as is common in the Evangelical church, came to speak about his experiences and to ask the congregation's support for his team's work by presenting a professionally produced, highly emotional multimedia and PowerPoint presentation. However, I was taken aback. He focused on the status of Christian missions to the Middle East and North Africa. Against a background of deep, somber music, slide after slide listed one nation after another—Ethiopia, Libya and the like—noting for each its total population and the corresponding number of "Christ followers." In some, that number was a hundred, or fifty, or even only five. In Egypt, the number he cited was in the low thousands. I thought about that. In a nation with deep Christian roots dating back to the early decades following Christ, home to tens of millions of people, this church leader considered only a relative handful to be true "Christ followers."

As I watched those estimates on the screen, I began to feel more and more uneasy. Why? Because that very morning's newscasts contained a report of a horrific attack upon hundreds of Coptic Christians protesting in their Egyptian homeland, with dozens martyred for their faith in Christ. And yet … and yet … this Evangelical missionary leader did not consider any of these souls to be "Christ followers." He presumed those who did not follow his form of Christianity were not true believers. He did not consider Roman Catholics, Eastern Orthodox, or members of the "mainstream" Protestant denominations to be true followers of Christ.

The Evangelicalism that this missionary professed considers being Christian as being *us against the world*. This attitude makes it difficult to present a positive view of the Church to non-believers. More importantly, this view might give the impression of a God who is not in control. Why, two thousand years after the resurrection, would there be so few true "Christ followers"? Jesus said the gates of hell would not stand against his Church, not that the gates of our church would stand defensively against the powers of hell. The difference is critical. We Christians are on the offensive. We are called to be bold, to attack evil where we see it, to help take back Christ's world, not to hunker down with a small group of like-minded people in an attempt simply to survive our time here on this planet. God's strength has led us from a pagan Roman world in which one small faithful Jewish nation followed the true God to a world where the greatest number of believers are Christian. Christ is reclaiming the world—his world. Christianity is on the rise and will be, with fits and starts, until his return. Are we to ignore and insult his power or his plans by looking at ourselves with the false pride of being one of a select few "true believers" scrambling day-by-day for survival in an evil world?

Concerning a man who was speaking in Jesus' name despite not being part of his inner circle of disciples, Jesus said "For whoever is not against us is for us" (Mk 9:40). Note the important direction to his thoughts. Jesus is saying in effect that we can unite with other Christians who are not *actively* against us and even learn from them, instead of trying to destroy their faith through our preference for what we consider to be our own "true faith." For whoever has *any* faith in Christ is not against us, and therefore can be, in the end, on our side.

We realize that God's grace is calling the hearts of every one of his children, and that we can find him and some portion of Christ's true "Church"—however small or ill-informed—in all men and women of good and honest will. We are certainly summoned to call them all, gently and lovingly, to a fuller and more complete saving faith in Jesus. But we do so by first acknowledging that *all* Christians are Christ-followers. Yes, we need a slightly confrontational attitude, recalling that we are the church militant. We cannot ease our way into heaven. We must join the fight, one that battles the evil we see within and without and strive to bring the greatest good—eternal life in Christ—to as many as possible. But we are to join in unity with all others, Catholic, Orthodox and Protestant alike, who are fighting this battle. In John 17 Jesus said that the great purpose of our unity here on Earth is to prove to disbelievers that the Father has truly sent him as Lord.

All Christians are Christ-followers and all human beings are children of God capable of receiving his grace. Some of my Evangelical friends might consider this attitude dangerously "open-minded." I do not. Let us not seek to invent heresies where they do not exist. Not every disagreement is a heresy, not every difference in opinion separates us from God and one another. That said, we must be willing to promote a pure sense of Christianity as we can, one that understands who God is and how Jesus came to be our Savior and our Lord. After all, it was the single-minded Christians of the first few centuries that eventually triumphed over the "open-minded" Roman Empire, for the betterment of the whole world both—in this life and the next.

Urgency

The Great Commission

Christians have slightly differing interpretations of Jesus' statement, "I am the way, and the truth, and the life. No one comes to the Father except through me" (Jn 14:6). They also differ about who should be considered a member of his Church. Does God save those who have heard and believed in Jesus, but not those who haven't, even if they have never had a chance to hear of Christ? Does God reward only those who respond to his call when they hear it, but punishes even those who have never *actively* deny him because they have not heard?

On the other hand, if we believe God offers salvation to those who have not actively denied Christ, are we then presuming that they can be saved without Jesus? Does a "merciful" position diminish the value of Christ's incarnation, death, and resurrection and so weaken the urgency of the Great Commission: "Go therefore and make disciples of all nations, baptizing them in the name of the Father and of the Son and of the Holy Spirit, and teaching them to obey everything that I have commanded you" (Mt 28: 18-20)? Jesus gave a clear directive that we bring his message to the entire world. Does a broader interpretation of salvation compromise the unique value of the Christian faith?

In the Catholic tradition, these issues can be summed up and reconciled in the words Jesus himself spoke as well as those of other writers (especially Paul). Through grace alone, *all* have within the desire to seek God. Jesus commanded that we "strive first for the kingdom of God and his righteousness, and all these things will be given to you as well" (Mt 6:33). No matter our identity or our background, the Spirit calls us to cooperate with the call that moves us toward God. If we decide freely to cooperate with that call, God will provide what we need to move toward the kingdom. We are to seek and knock and ask, and the door will be opened, the knock will be answered. We will find what we seek.

We Christians are fortunate to have heard the full truth of the gospel. If we remain in a state of grace, we are among the elect, blessed to have followed God's call. We must hold fast to faith, never lose it, never throw it away. God has already given us what we have sought, has opened the door upon which we have knocked. To embrace any other philosophy or belief is to turn our backs on God and *actively* deny his grace and his call to salvation.

Our Personal Commission

The Evangelical churches I have attended offer the laity unquestionably superior training in the practice of reaching out to unbelievers because they maintain a clear focus upon the Great Commission. They are serious about the laity's role in what St. John Paul called the "New Evangelization." The same Evangelical church that hosted a clearly anti-Catholic missionary sets aside three or four weeks, usually after the rush of Christmas and New Year, for a guest speaker. One speaker, a former non-believer, had become a professor at a leading Christian college. He is one of the most engaging, funny, and thoughtful speakers I have ever heard. He presented a simple technique to develop our abilities to share our Christian story with the world, specifically the story about how Christ became the Lord of our lives.

He used the biblical story in which St. Paul related his own background to the King Agrippa (Acts 26). He showed how we Christians ought to prepare a short, two-minute presentation during which we can share our own life story with non-believers we might encounter in our daily lives. He warned that, if we were converts (to his form of Evangelicalism), we should not denigrate the church which we believe failed us prior to becoming Evangelical, nor should we present a memorized series of bible citations or a "Cliff-notes" version of theology. No, he said, we must realize that non-believers must first understand, emotionally, how coming to Christ can heal them and fulfill their lives. And what better way to do that than to describe how Christ did these things for us?

He suggested we focus on three simple things. First, what was happening inside us when we committed ourselves to Christ? Second, how did we experience his call? Third, what has happened to us since? He suggested we write these things down, rereading and revising our story until we could relate it simply and quickly. He asked us to practice it by ourselves or, if possible, with another believer. We were then to look for opportunities in our daily lives to share this story with others.

How ... simple.

And yet, in fifty years of Catholic life I had never once been given such a simple, personal method of effective evangelization. I was never taught how to share my faith story with others, yet Catholics need to do exactly this, understanding and expressing our personal commitment to Christ as well as a short, heartfelt description of the good we have found in his Church. We should acknowledge that we who are "lifelong" Catholics have extraordinary stories, as powerful as any adult convert to the faith or our "born again" Evangelical friends. Stability, peace, love, acceptance, and deep—blessedly deep—roots; the benefits of lifelong faith in God, along with the moments of pain and of joy when we felt Christ come alive within us.

Tradition: A Practical Matter

The Christian Church, a living body, has multiple sources supporting its life: believers who have come to know Jesus before us, a core of fundamental beliefs defined through its Tradition, the generally accepted interpretation of scripture and understanding of the faith passed down from the apostles and those who have succeeded them. Most of all, its life is inspired by the ongoing guidance of the Holy Spirit, promised by Jesus until the end of the age.

Some Christians claim faith in Jesus Christ as their savior and go no deeper. Others focus on routines such as attending weekly worship but neglect developing a relationship with Christ, presuming that rituals will gain them eternal life. In his first letter to the community at Corinth, Paul warned about both incomplete approaches to the faith: "And so, brothers and sisters, I could not speak to you as spiritual people, but rather as people of the flesh, as infants in Christ. I fed you with milk, not solid food, for you were not ready for solid food" (1 Cor 3:1-2). Paul began preaching the gospel by focusing on the "milk" of the faith, on the straightforward idea of accepting Christ's forgiveness and baptism into his Church. The Apostle's letter continued, explaining the way men and women should relate to one another, the nature of the Lord's Supper, and proper behavior at that sacred event. And he concludes with these words: "About the other things I will give instructions when I come" (1 Cor 11:34).

Here we see two realities regarding the infant Church. First, Paul and his fellow apostles assumed responsibility to instruct the local churches. Second, and more importantly, Paul gave—or intended to give—instructions to the local church not only through letters but in person. Paul must have considered his written words worthwhile, but he also realized the importance of face to face instruction and the limitations, especially at that time, of exhaustive written instructions.

The fundamental beliefs of the Church are formulated in written creeds, but the Church also provides other "solid food." I accept the Catholic Church's expression of faith because I believe that following Christ's ascension into heaven, the Holy Spirit has guided this body of believers. The Holy Spirit instructs and protects the Church, correcting misdirected heresies and affirming authentic belief. The Bible does not list an expiration date for the work of the Holy Spirit. Those who say they believe all truth comes only from the Bible confine the work of the Spirit to only helping us decipher those words. Jesus told the apostles, "I will ask the Father, and he will give you another Advocate, to be with you forever.... The Advocate, the Holy Spirit, whom the Father will send in my name, will teach you everything, and remind you of all that I have said to you" (Jn 14: 16, 26). In giving them "authority," Jesus was preparing a living church to survive an ever-changing world.

Over the past several years, as I have dug deeper into issues that at first glance seem unimportant to my eternal salvation, I felt the hunger for more of the Christian faith's "solid food." The Church's faith and logic on all issues, great and small, brought me deep comfort. I have come to accept its doctrine not as a matter of blind obedience but because I have faith that the Church can logically, historically, and biblically justify the truths it teaches. I desire to pass on to my children a faith founded upon the bedrock of the Church's two millennia of wisdom, God-given wisdom that will strengthen them throughout their lives. And when they encounter the difficult ethical decisions everyone who takes faith seriously must face, they can hold on to a sure rock, the teachings of the Church, instead of their own momentary feelings and desires.

There are two issues of my personal Catholic journey I have always struggled with, though I never felt either issue stood at the core of the gospel message. Challenged by my new faith family, I had to search for the truth in these areas. And, as I grew in knowledge, I also grew in confidence in my Catholic faith and in my desire for Christian unity.

Mary

I used to be uncomfortable with some Catholic teachings (or what I understood the teachings to be) regarding Mary. As a child, I learned to say the Hail Mary as an evening prayer. I learned how to recite the rosary, but I really didn't think too much about Mary one way or the other. I knew the Church didn't teach us to "worship" her, but the passion with which some Catholics regard the Blessed Mother made me uncomfortable.

As an adult, my interaction with Evangelicals made me aware that Catholic teaching and practice concerning Mary are at the root of some of the deepest rifts within the Christian family. At first I thought the objections to Catholic beliefs and practices concerning Mary were silly. It seemed both intellectually honest and deeply scriptural that we ask Christ's earthly mother to pray *for* us and that we honor her humility and dutiful service to God. The problems and causes for disunity, I came to realize, lay in differences in how we understand what it means to *pray*.

Catholics understand the word "pray"—as in "pray to Mary" or "pray to the saints"—to mean something different than do Evangelicals. Catholics consider prayer to be communication. Prayer is speaking to God, and (hopefully) listening to God's response. The Catholic Mass is marked by an atmosphere more subdued than at most Evangelical worship services, a quiet reverence that allows personal and communal prayer (communication) with the Lord. Most Evangelicals, however, associate "prayer" primarily with worship. Their services are louder, full of song, full of hand-raising and spontaneous "amens."

So, when Catholics say they "pray" to Mary, Evangelicals naturally see this prayer in terms of worship, which of course any thoughtful Christian would consider idolatry. Some Evangelical preachers maintain that Catholic clergy teach the faithful to "worship" Mary and the saints, whereas the Bible clearly teaches we should worship only God: "You shall not make for yourself an idol, whether in the form of anything that is in heaven above, or that is on the earth beneath, or that is in the water under the earth. You shall not bow down to them or worship them; for I the Lord your God am a jealous God" (Ex 20:4-5).

But if Catholics claim only to be communicating with Mary, what exactly is being communicated? We are communicating requests that she *intercede* (pray *for* us) with God on our behalf, just as Christians of all denominations and backgrounds are taught to pray to God for each other's provision. If we flawed human beings can pray for each other, then it only stands to reason we can also call upon those already in God's eternal presence—and first among that heavenly band must be Jesus' mother—to intercede for us.

This seemed an obvious reality and truth, but it was not until I attended Evangelical services that I came to a full understanding of the issue, and of the solution. It is only through these personal life experiences and the willingness to search out the views of the "other" that I found a path around which Christians might understand each other and unite.

Evangelicals are often taught that correct prayer is done in four steps, outlined by the word, *ACTS*. We first **A**dore (worship) God, which puts us in the proper humble relation with our creator. Then, we **C**onfess our sins to God, as alone can forgive us. We then give him **T**hanks for those things he has blessed us with out of his own power. Finally, we ourselves **S**upplicate, requesting the blessings we hope to receive through his love, mercy and power. One common theme connects these four points. They all equate prayer with the things that can be offered only to God.

When Catholics say we "pray" to Mary or to a saint, Evangelicals assume we are praying according to their four steps and, therefore, rightly object to such a practice. But Catholics do not **A**dore (worship) Mary in prayer. We do not **C**onfess our sins to her seeking her forgiveness. We do not **T**hank her for providing us something through her own power (though we might thank her for interceding for us with God who provided out of his own power). Finally, we do not Supplicate before her as if we believe that she, with her own inherent power, can grant us anything. We know that we only ask for intercession to the Father in the name of her Son, so that God in his power will grant what we need and desire.

Explained like this, framing the discussion in the way already familiar to Evangelicals, is helpful in conveying our true meaning and build unity within the body of Christ.

Purgatory

Another doctrine that divides Catholics and Evangelicals is purgatory. All Christians believe whoever repents and asks for forgiveness in the name of Jesus will enter heaven. In Catholic teaching, purgatory is a necessary step in the journey from earthly life to heavenly life.

In Martin Luther's day, the sale of indulgences, so closely tied to the concept of purgatory, had become scandalously corrupt. The Reformers were right to criticize the practice, but in their zeal they denied the Church's long-held tradition concerning purgatory. As the Reformation developed, enmity caused Protestants to lose something precious of the faith. This was beyond unfortunate for, even in their own time, the early Reformers were acknowledged by the Council of Trent, which took steps to stop the abuses of the sale of indulgences.

Catholic doctrine holds that at death some are capable of the beatific vision (being in the presence of

God in heaven) while others who die in a state of grace—with their sins forgiven and destined for heaven—need purification ("purgatory" is a place or condition of purification) before they can be ready to face God.

Some Evangelicals misunderstand Catholic teaching. They suppose that Catholics understand hell to be eternal torment, yet non-believers and the non-unrepentant can still escape this by being "purchased" out of damnation not through their own belief in Jesus as their savior, but because friends and family say enough prayers or perform enough rituals or give enough money to the Church. They believe that in purgatory Catholics teach a "second chance" for those who died enemies of Christ.

The truth is, Catholics do *not* believe purgatory "saves"; it is not a "second chance" after death. Purgatory only "purifies." The doctrine of purgatory holds that after death a believer whose soul is still damaged and impure needs a period of "cleansing." It has never been specified what this cleansing entails or how long it endures, so there is no conflict between the doctrine of purgatory and scripture. This doctrine, however, is both biblical and logical. Clearly, God calls all who are saved through faith in Christ to be with him forever in heaven. Yet anything less than perfection cannot endure the perfection of heaven. As we read in Revelation, nothing impure can reside in the presence of God, and certainly not for eternity. Protestants and Catholics alike realize that many, many souls who did evil on earth may enter heaven by throwing themselves upon the mercy of Christ before death.

But who can enter heaven? If we beg mercy in Jesus' name. God forgives our sins, but we remain the same souls. After death, we still are who we are, the same deeply flawed soul, fallen but redeemed. Take for example the universally held personification of evil, Adolf Hitler. If at the very last moment of his life he had begged for Christ's saving mercy, Christian doctrine holds that even a person who has done such monstrously evil deeds would be saved. From their perspective, Evangelicals would have to say that upon his death a repentant Hitler would go directly and permanently into the presence of God, his dirty soul covered by a spotless wedding gown provided by the Son. But could Hitler, stained by false pride, murder, beastly deeds, really endure standing before the All-Good, the All-True, the All-Beautiful? God is not a liar and cannot lie even to himself about the souls in his eternal presence.

However, purgatory is not just purification for God's sake. It is a great blessing given by God, who wants us to enjoy his presence to the full. Our evil deeds and pride cannot affect God in heaven; we creatures cannot affect our eternal Creator, but we likewise cannot share eternity if still marked with the effects of our impurity, pride, and anger. Not only should we grudgingly accept purgatory; we should thank God for such a blessing. Catholic doctrine holds that the soul of a sinner who has so much to repent of would feel unworthy and would actually desire to be cleansed before being able to enjoy God forever.

Who's Wrong?

I did not write this book either as an iron-clad statement of the true faith or with any pretense that I know it all. I write only from my singular position as a Catholic living with a positive outlook toward my new Evangelical environment, and a person exposed to Evangelical thought who has found my Catholic roots more and more representative of true and fundamental Christianity. I live in the unconventional position of a father desperate to share the reasons why I remain a Catholic with my children, while respecting that their own futures in the faith are still to be determined. Mary and the doctrine of purgatory are among those considerations which led me to respect the traditional teachings of the Church more deeply. When our natural inclination is to believe one thing while the Church teaches another, we need *not* ask why the Church can't change. Our first move must always be to question our reactions and instincts and, in all truth and sincerity, seek the depths of the Church's teachings to put *our* thoughts into proper perspective and adjust *our* thinking.

Catholics and Evangelicals alike applaud Origen as one of the greatest (though not perfect) Christian teachers after the apostles. Origen said, "If I do anything contrary to the discipline of the Church or the rule laid down in the Gospels—if I give offense (through my teaching) to you and to the Church—then I hope the whole Church will unite with one consent and cast me off" (*Homily to Joshua* 7.6).

He clearly understood the dangers of heresy within Christ's family, and our tendency toward disunity.

Chapter 5

Worship and Sacrament

The Mass

St. Justin to Emperor Antoninus Pius (AD 155)

On the day we call the day of the sun, all who dwell in the city or country gather in the same place.

The memoirs of the apostles and the writings of the prophets are read, as much as time permits.

When the reader has finished, he who presides over those gathered admonishes and challenges them to imitate these beautiful things.

Then we all rise together and offer prayers for ourselves ... and for all others, wherever they may be, so that we may be found righteous by our life and actions, and faithful to the commandments, so as to obtain eternal salvation.

When the prayers are concluded we exchange the kiss.

Then someone brings bread and a cup of water and wine mixed together to him who presides over the brethren.

He takes them and offers praise and glory to the Father of the universe, through the name of the Son and of the Holy Spirit and for a considerable time he gives thanks (in Greek: *eucharistian*) that we have been judged worthy of these gifts.

When he has concluded the prayers and thanksgivings, all present give voice to an acclamation by saying: "Amen."

When he who presides has given thanks and the people have responded, those whom we call deacons give to those present the "eucharisted" bread, wine and water and take them to those who are absent. (*Catechism of the Catholic Church*, 1345)

St. Justin, a convert to Christianity and a forceful apologist in the early Church who died for his faith, wrote this account almost two thousand years ago. Twenty-first century Catholics recognize this as a description of the contemporary Catholic Mass, which maintains a tradition of worship that extends back to the time of Christ himself.

All Christians, Catholic and Evangelical alike, seek and may find eternal life with our Father. We love our Lord, love our Father, and break out into Spirit-driven acts of worship. But is it important what form our worship takes? Is it critical that we maintain a form of worship consistent with what our ancestors have done? Can those whose practices differ from the ones I am accustomed to still be called "Christian"?

I have benefitted from the Evangelical services I've attended. Though a lifelong Catholic, those services helped sustain and even deepen my faith. So, should I maintain that the Catholic way of worshiping God is the correct, and perhaps, *only* way acceptable to God? Can I say that one form of Christian worship is more fundamental, more in tune with God's desire? The more I consider this issue, the more I realize the God of the Old Testament was (and therefore is) *very* interested in how people worship. Even a cursory reading of the Old testament offers a clear, detailed description of what God desired for his people.

Such preferences certainly do not affect God. What vestments were worn or what instruments were played made little difference to an eternal Lord. God was not happier with his people if the sacrifices offered at an Old Testament feast were doubled, or halved. His prophet even says explicitly that the sacrifices themselves are not what matters: "What do I care for the multitude of your sacrifices? says the LORD. I have had enough of whole-burnt rams and fat of fatlings; In the blood of calves, lambs, and goats I find no pleasure" (Is 1:11). No, requirements are set forth in those scriptures—whether circumcision or dietary restrictions or the celebration of certain festivals—because proper worship and other religious practices help *us*.

Earlier we looked at the creeds and how they developed. The same fathers of the church who formulated these statements of orthodox Christianity also followed and taught a certain pattern of worship. Christians ought to consider that the form they practiced and the theology they found within these practices carries a special validity, inspired by the Holy Spirit. For example, Irenaeus (born 130 AD) in *Against Heresies* wrote:

> ... the blessed Paul declares in his Epistle to the Ephesians, that "we are members of His body, of His flesh, and of His bones." He does not speak these words of some spiritual and invisible man, for a spirit has not bones nor flesh; but [he refers to] that dispensation [by which the Lord became] an actual man, consisting of flesh, and nerves, and bones,—that [flesh] which is nourished by the cup which is His blood, and receives increase from the bread which is His body. And just as a cutting from the vine planted in the ground fructifies in its season, or as a corn of wheat falling into the earth and becoming decomposed, rises with manifold increase by the Spirit of God, who contains all things, and then, through the wisdom of God, serves for the use of men, and having received the Word of God, becomes the Eucharist, which is the body and blood of Christ.[11]

---

11. *The Writings of Irenaeus* (Edinburgh: Aeterna Press, 2015), 358.

Chapter 3 discussed the Bible, the fundamental document of Christian faith. Here, we will consider the sacraments and the Mass, the fundamental Christian forms of worship, our primary ways we encounter Jesus. The more I have explored the Mass, the more clearly I understood how the Mass reflects the style and substance of the Bible. Even more striking—something I never considered before being challenged by my Evangelical experiences—is how much the Bible follows the Mass.

It only makes sense.

If those who wrote the New Testament texts worshiped Jesus in a certain way in the early Church, then those practices would certainly shape their writings about our Lord and the Christian faith. For example, John 6 recounts Christ's teaching regarding eating his body and drinking his blood:

> Very truly, I tell you, unless you eat the flesh of the Son of Man and drink his blood, you have no life in you.... Those who eat my flesh and drink my blood abide in me, and I in them.... This is the bread that came down from heaven, not like that which your ancestors ate, and they died. But the one who eats this bread will live forever. (Jn 6: 53, 56, 58)

Fifty years or so after the resurrection, when he composed his Gospel, John would have conveyed to the freshly-born Christian community what Jesus said and did regarding the Eucharist. It is likely that John's account reflects the Eucharistic celebration already in

practice within that community. We see that in his letters
to the Corinthians Paul also discusses that celebration.

Many Evangelical churches approach the connection between scripture and worship from a different
perspective. They seek to bring back to life a "perfect
and fundamental" church and worship through a literal
reading of various parts of the New Testament. Such an
approach can be beneficial if there is agreement on how
scripture is to be interpreted. A deep examination of
scripture may enable Christians to clarify religious ceremonies that over millennia have taken on non-scriptural
dimensions. But renewing or recreating Christian worship through a re-reading of scripture carries the risk of
inferring a meaning that the original text did not intend.
All writings, including inspired ones, reflect the cultural
context in which they were composed. In addition, the
very early Church, comprised of the Twelve and a few
followers, would surely look and act differently than
the contemporary Christian Church, which numbers
over two billion adherents scattered throughout the
world. Those wanting to recreate what the first generation of Christians experienced need to acknowledge that
those members of the Church did not possess the New
Testament in any form. They only had the apostles.

The Mass is the primary experience of the Catholic
Christian. Through it the faithful learn doctrine, build
community, and enter into proper and humble worship of God. Any church needs a fundamental means of
securing and building the faith as its members make their
way through life, as well as a way of passing on the faith
to future generations. For two millennia and more, the

Mass has served these purposes. All Christians—those who worship at the Mass and those whose worship takes other forms—are brothers and sisters in faith. Through my experience in the Evangelical church, a Catholic like me has come to appreciate the depth and beauty of the Mass; my Evangelical brothers and sisters have the same opportunity to reflect on and appreciate their own practices by entering the worship experience of Catholics, their brothers and sisters in Christ.

Form of Evangelical Services

At worship, Evangelicals praise God. Through the praise of any Christian, God grants us a change to not reflect upon our problems but upon him. As C.S. Lewis said in *The Four Loves,* "We are mirrors whose brightness, if we are bright, is wholly derived from the sun that shines upon us."[12] When we see only God's brightness; we do not see the darkness of our shadows.

Despite my initial misgivings, in the services at the two congregations my family belonged to, I found God among these Christians as I always found him among my fellow Catholics. There are two unfortunate stereotypes of American Evangelicals: rowdy, hands-in-the-air while you pray, speak-in-tongues types; or dour "Bible-thumpers" calling down fire and brimstone upon sinners. To be sure, both have some basis in fact. But most Evangelical pastors are thoughtful people sincerely trying to obey God and their congregations are likewise people

---

12. C.S. Lewis, *The Four Loves* (New York: Harcourt Brace, 1960), 131.

who love Christ. Their services and practices reveal the
wisdom the Spirit has provided.

Evangelical services contain two parts. The "worship" portion includes energetic and often inspiring communal song. This opening part of the Sunday services
was sometimes tailored to the principal audience. For the
"gray hairs," traditional organ and choir music; for the
younger members, renditions of fast-paced music with
full rock bands—ripping guitar solos and strong per-
cussion. Younger Evangelicals do not worship through
quiet prayer and reflection, but in Old Testament,
"David dancing before the Ark" styles that convey love,
adoration, and joy. The enthusiasm they "feel" for the
Lord wipes away disappointment and worldly worries.
They focus on the exhilaration all Christians ought to
feel because they are redeemed from sin and headed for
heavenly bliss.

At first, the rock and roll energy directed toward
younger congregants felt inappropriate to my Catholic
ears; the services seemed to lack holiness and a focus
upon the Lord. I found the sheer volume of a rock band
highly bothersome, particularly during a religious experience in which we may be feeling the purifying guilt of
our sins, or the deep pain of a loss. To drive away the
white-haired crowd by offering only the louder music
that attracts the young also damages one of the main
goals of church, to safely bring believers to their Savior
up to and through the point of death. But others find
that the slow melodies of the classics suppress their joy
in the presence of God. Never should a child of God be
lost to boredom. I came to realize that Evangelicals give

glory to God through liveliness and passion. What at first seemed showy and secular allows congregants to shake off their daily troubles and prepare for the glory and joy in heaven to come.

Some Evangelicals surely would be put off by the slow organ keyboarding at most Catholic Masses and the sparse number of parishioners who join in singing the older, more traditional songs. They would be right to be concerned, for the Mass is supposed to be a true celebration, a direct physical contact with our Lord and Savior in the Eucharist. Catholics, indeed all Christians, ought to be like the very stones Jesus said "would shout out" in his presence (Lk 19:40). That said, the musical tradition Catholics maintain was also important to the early Reformers. Some Evangelical preachers today prefer "carols and hymns." They believe the non-traditional has no part in a true Christian service. Some Reformation figures—indeed, Calvin himself—banned singing at worship services altogether. Musical choices, then, are clearly a matter of taste, not doctrine. They ought not divide the Christian family.

Catholics could use a musical "refresher," however, although not going so far as to place a band center stage and pushing aside the Mass. Like Evangelical churches, Catholic parishes can—and do—offer a variety of worship services each weekend, a combination of modern and classical music so that every parishioner can come closer to God and be moved to go forth and live their faith. Catholics possess musical talents equal to those of Evangelicals. Without doubt, every Catholic parish has a young drummer, a middle-aged electric guitarist, and everyone else needed to make the Mass more engaging and uplifting.

At a recent Easter Mass at my parents' parish in West Linn, Oregon, the songs were identical to those at our Evangelical services in the Midwest. The tempo was slower and the instrumentation more traditional, but the livelier songs engaged the congregation. Rarely have I seen so many Catholics singing with such enthusiasm! "Modern" music reflects the culture in which we live and engages our children. Instead of their daily—and nightly—diet of secular songs, I would prefer God-filled songs at the tips of their tongues. It *is* possible. Much is played on Evangelical radio stations—Christian pop and Christian rock—as well as recordings by Christian singers and bands that equal or surpass much of today's "commercial" music.

Songs I learned when I was young, such as John Michael Talbott's "On Eagles' Wings," or "Amazing Grace," still sustain me through life's events and challenges. And yet many songs from at our Evangelical services have also burned into my heart. For example, I never fail to be moved by MercyMe's "I Can Only Imagine":

> I can only imagine what it will be like,
> when I walk by Your side ...
> I can only imagine,
> what my eyes will see,
> when Your Face is before me!
> I can only imagine. I can only imagine.

Surrounded by Your Glory,
what will my heart feel?
Will I dance for you, Jesus?
Or in awe of You, be still?
Will I stand in Your presence,
or to my knees will I fall?
Will I sing "Hallelujah!"?
Will I be able to speak at all?
I can only imagine! I can only imagine!

After engaging the congregation with music, an Evangelical service generally proceeds to communal prayer, often free-form with frequent scriptural allusions, offered by the music leader or pastor. Although I always found this form of prayer to be sincere, at first it did not sit well with my Catholic sensibilities. Certain catchphrases—"loving on you," or frequent repetitions of "Father" or "Lord"—annoyed me. When I find myself resisting such prayers, however, I try to remember that I am recoiling not from the prayer itself, but from its unfamiliarity.

Some significant differences between prayers at Mass and those at an Evangelical worship service are not simply a matter of taste or custom, however. Catholics emphasize communal prayer in which the parishioners recite together the same words. During their services Evangelicals rarely pray in such fashion. At every Catholic Mass, for example, the entire people recites "I confess to almighty God ... " and "Holy, holy, holy Lord God of hosts ... " and "By your cross and resurrection you have set us free; you are the savior of the world" and

"Our Father, who art in heaven ... ," words Jesus taught the apostles when they asked him how to pray. The fact that Matthew and Luke both include this prayer in their Gospels suggests that those early Christian communities in which they lived also prayed in the same way.

So, too, almost every Catholic knows the Nicene Creed because they recite it at every Sunday Mass. This creed—written under the inspiration of the Holy Spirit— enumerates fundamental orthodox Christian beliefs. By reciting it together every week, Catholics around the world commit to memory these basic, deeply scriptural truths that are part of the Church's tradition. Also, (and, sad to say, I never really understood this until my Catholic beliefs were challenged) biblical concepts permeate what Catholics recite or sing at Mass. Evangelicals, were they to experience their Catholic brothers and sisters at worship, would recognize how the Mass is deeply Christ-centered and profoundly Bible-focused.

Unlike Protestant or Evangelical services, the Catholic Mass does not center only on the Bible. It does not center on the teachings of Paul or Peter or Luke or John. It focuses instead upon the life—still among us—of Jesus. To paraphrase the eloquence of C.S. Lewis, it is not so much the teachings of Christ that matter, but Christ himself that matters. It is not our mental capacity to understand the details of how we are saved through Christ that matters as much as the faith that we are not only saved by Christ but freed and guided to live better lives here on earth.

In like manner, Masses do not focus upon the pastor, or the sermon, or the choir. They do not resemble pep rallies or college lectures. The Mass is the public, and yet also private, expression of Christ's sacrifice and his continuing, material presence in the Eucharist. The marquee outside a Catholic church does not advertise the pastor's name, nor the title of his next sermon—that is not what the Mass is about, nor who the Mass is for. Typically, Catholics do not applaud the musicians or the choir. At Mass, dignitaries are not offered the pulpit. They remain within the body of worshipers whose dignity derives from Christ's, represented upon his cross at the focal point of the church. The talent of those who sing and play and preach is offered up as a sacrifice to the one who provided the talent.

What am I Seeing?

Evangelicals who wish to accept Catholics as fellow brothers and sisters in Christ might be aided by an explanation of the Mass. And Catholics, so accustomed to the Mass, can benefit from a better understanding of "what am I seeing?"

A non-believer who attends Evangelical services has the comfort of easily understanding the service—songs of praise followed by a "lecture." Non-believers who attend a Mass need an explanation of its elements. Perhaps if Catholic churches offered a monthly "outreach Mass" that includes a few extra minutes of explanation, parishioners would find it easier to introduce those unfamiliar with Catholic worship to the richness of the Mass. And Catholics would be reenergized by their primary event in their faith.

Mass begins with a processional song. Led by a crucifix, focusing upon the sacrifice of our Lord, the priest enters the sanctuary, marking the transition from the world's time and space to God's. After inviting the congregation to sign themselves "In the name of the Father, and of the Son, and of the Holy Spirit," and invoking "The grace of our Lord Jesus Christ and the love of God and the fellowship of the Holy Spirit be with you all," he reads a brief gathering prayer based on scripture. The priest then leads the congregation in a "penitential" rite to acknowledge our sins and ask for the Lord's forgiveness and grace.

The Mass then moves into the "celebration (or "liturgy") of the word." Every Mass—every single Mass—contains two or three readings from scripture. Although I have found the scriptural reflection by Evangelical preachers sometimes more in-depth and emotionally forceful, the Mass is consistent in citing scripture to develop a theme taken from Christ's life, with readings from the Old Testament, the Epistles, and the Gospels. This is part of the depth and beauty of the Mass. At our Evangelical megachurch, we once spent *twenty-six-weeks* discussing only the Epistle to the Ephesians. I achieved a far greater understanding of Ephesians than ever before. But for that entire span—almost half a year—we heard not one word from the Old Testament, some part of which is presented at every Sunday Mass. Much more troubling to me, for *half a year* we did not read or hear a single direct word from our Lord. Not in the readings, not in any communal prayer. Not that every word in scripture is not inspired, but as a Christian I hunger first and foremost to focus on what Christ said, taught, and did. To that end, every Mass includes a reading from one of the Gospels, usually including an event from Jesus' life and ministry.

Following the scripture readings, the priest gives a "homily" that explores the theme contained in the readings. This discussion "unpacks" scripture, but also is an occasion for passing along and explaining church doctrine. After the homily, the congregation recites the creed, which for 1700 years has defined orthodox Christianity.

The community then praises God and offers prayers of petition for their own spiritual and physical well-being and for the world's, particularly for those who suffer from illness or who have died. Then "gifts" are brought forward—the bread and wine that will be offered and consecrated, as well as money to meet the needs of the local community and the Church as a whole. After the priest formally offers the bread and wine to God, we join our earthly voices to those of the heavenly choir which today, this *very instant* and forever more praises the Lord as we see reflected in the Book of Revelation. "Holy, holy, holy the Lord God the Almighty, who was and is and is to come" (Rev 4:8).

The focus of the Mass now turns from God's written word to the *Word* of God. Directly, wholly, and firmly, attention is focused upon Christ and his sacrifice. The bread and wine are "eucharisted" as the priest pronounces, virtually word for word, what Christ said over the bread and the chalice at the Last Supper. The prayers that follow remind us—the very sinners Jesus came to redeem, members of the present congregation as well as members of the Body of Christ throughout this world and the next—of the significance of what we are doing, what we are about to receive in the Eucharist. We recognize our dependence upon Jesus and his grace.

As a community, we then obey Jesus' command and recite the Lord's Prayer. We greet each other with the sign of peace, a tradition going back at least to the middle of the first century that includes the words that the Resurrected Lord spoke to his apostles as he entered the Upper Room, "Peace be with you." Then, before presenting ourselves to receive the Eucharist, we repeat together what the Roman centurion said to Jesus: "Lord, I am not worthy to have you come under my roof; but only speak the word, and [I] ... will be healed" (Mt 8:8).

And then—then we touch the infinite. We receive our Lord in the Eucharist.

Finally, we are dismissed with a closing prayer and a benediction, strengthened with Christ within us to bring the Word of God to the world.

The Eucharist

"Very truly, I tell you, whoever believes has eternal life. I am the bread of life. Your ancestors ate the manna in the wilderness, and they died. This is the bread that comes down from heaven, so that one may eat of it and not die. I am the living bread that came down from heaven. Whoever eats of this bread will live forever; and the bread that I will give for the life of the world is my flesh."

The Jews then disputed among themselves, saying, "How can this man give us his flesh to eat?" So Jesus said to them, "Very truly, I tell you, unless you eat the flesh of the Son of Man and drink his blood, you have no life in you. Those who eat my flesh and drink my blood have eternal life, and I will raise them up on the last day; for my flesh is true food and my blood is true drink. Those who eat my flesh and drink my blood abide in me, and I in them. Just as the living Father sent me, and I live because of the Father, so whoever eats me will live because of me. This is the bread that came down from heaven, not like that which your ancestors ate, and they died. But the one who eats this bread will live forever." He said these things while he was teaching in the synagogue at Capernaum.

When many of his disciples heard it, they said, "This teaching is difficult; who can accept it?" But Jesus, being aware that his disciples were complaining about it, said to them, "Does this offend you? Then what if you were to see the Son of Man ascending to where he was before? It is the spirit that gives life; the flesh is useless. The words that I have spoken to you are spirit and life. But among you there are some who do not believe." For Jesus knew from the first who were the ones that did not believe, and who was the one that would betray him. And he said, "For this

reason I have told you that no one can come
to me unless it is granted by the Father."

Because of this many of his disciples turned
back and no longer went about with him. So
Jesus asked the twelve, "Do you also wish to
go away?" Simon Peter answered him, "Lord,
to whom can we go? You have the words of
eternal life." (Jn 6:47-68)

Whoever, therefore, eats the bread or drinks
the cup of the Lord in an unworthy manner
will be answerable for the body and blood
of the Lord.[28] Examine yourselves, and only
then eat of the bread and drink of the cup.[29]
For all who eat and drink **without discerning the body**, eat and drink judgement
against themselves. [30]For this reason, many
of you are weak and ill, and some have died.
(1 Cor 11:27-30, bold added.)

The quotation from St. Justin that began this
chapter reflects the form and function of the Mass and
the Eucharistic celebration as they have existed since the
beginning of Christianity. The quotation above from the
Gospel of John is a warrant for Catholic belief that Jesus
is physically present in the Eucharist. In the consecrated
bread and wine is received not just the spirit of Christ,
but his entire body and blood, soul and divinity, which
he shares with those who partake of it. The Eucharist is
not secondary, an act performed merely "in memory" of
Jesus as it seems to be at the Evangelical worship services

I've experienced. It is a physical sign of our salvation and the greatest source of our strength.

The Eucharist, or the "Lord's Table," both signify the great action of God in our world for us, sinful people. Regrettably, the Eucharist has also been used to divide the Church. There are two principal arguments against the Catholic interpretation of the sixth chapter of John's Gospel. These arguments are presented here not meant to diminish the sincerity and faith of those who do not accept the Real Presence, but to demonstrate the logic and scriptural basis for Catholic belief.

Some note that Jesus' words in John's sixth chapter come long before the final institution of the Eucharist at the Last Supper. How can his words be then taken to refer to a future event? But throughout the Gospels, Jesus predicts and discusses future events. Well before his own crucifixion he tells his listeners they must carry their own crosses—tools for execution—and follow him. How strange these words must have been! Yet he told them about the cross so that, following his resurrection, they would remember and understand the universal call to sacrifice for the Lord. Jesus also predicted the meaning of the Eucharist long before he held up the bread and wine at the Last Supper.

Second, some argue that at the end of the chapter when some "turned back and no longer went about with him," it only means that these people were upset Jesus was not going to multiply loaves and fishes again to give them a free lunch. However, there is no indication of this complaint in John 6. The text instead suggests that those who left Jesus took his words to mean that the bread and wine would literally become his flesh and blood. Described as "disciples," these people were Christ's followers and seem not to have taken issue with other things Jesus taught, but this new mandate was too much for them. The Jews at that event also understood Jesus was not talking about his body and blood figuratively: "The Jews then disputed among themselves, saying, 'How can this man give us his flesh to eat?'"

Despite the Jews' misgivings and his own disciples' brewing rebellion, Jesus did not soften his statements. He answered, "Very truly, I tell you, unless you eat the flesh of the Son of Man and drink his blood, you have no life in you. 54Those who *eat my flesh* and *drink my blood* [emphasis added] have eternal life, and I will raise them up on the last day; 55for my flesh is true food and my blood is true drink. Those who eat my flesh and drink my blood abide in me, and I in them." Moreover, the disciples—even John himself—seem to share the concerns of the Jewish leaders. "When many of his disciples heard it, they said, 'This teaching is difficult; who can accept it?'"

Even if Christians today cannot bring themselves to agree on this critical issue, no one can read this passage and, in good faith, suppose Catholics to be insincere or biblically unfounded in their understanding and their celebration of the Eucharist. Many Evangelical/Protestant doctrines are based upon a reading of Biblical passages much less clear than John's sixth chapter, such as belief in being "born again" that is based upon Jesus' single statement with Nicodemus in the third chapter of the same Gospel. It is significant that in his Gospel, the last to be written, John chose to focus on these words of Jesus regarding his body and blood, presenting them so unambiguously. Several decades after the crucifixion, John was reflecting what was significant within the nascent Christian community and what was not.

During that last holy meal Christ fortified himself with bread and wine, and down through the centuries he has continued to convey his own strength by means of those same elements. Just as the Last Supper strengthened him against that long, lonely night on Gethsemane and the agony of crucifixion, so we are strengthened against the inevitable trials in our own lives.

Two Thousand Years

After my family attended Evangelical services, I struggled to decide whether to bring my kids to Mass without my wife, or to join her so we could attend Evangelical services as a family. I tried to accept all I could that was positive from the Evangelical services, met several sincere Christians, was enthused by the unconventional church music, and learned how to study the Bible at a deeper and more precise level. But when I saw serving trays placed upon a table at the front of the stage, signifying the monthly "Lord's Table," the Evangelical celebration of Communion, I felt a dagger of concern pierce my soul. The elders passed out two little plastic cups, one holding a tiny cracker, the other an ounce or so of grape juice. With lights dimmed, the pastor would pray over the table, sometimes using the words Jesus said in the Upper Room, the same words Catholic priests pronounce at every Mass. The pastor once concluded: "This Table is and has been at the heart of Evangelical Christianity for the past two thousand years." I almost fell out of my comfortably padded seat!

In one sense, his words bore a truth greater than he may have intended. The first and most evangelical of all Christian Churches, the Church that birthed the four evangelists as well as Paul and, for the next fifteen hundred years, other great leaders and writers and teachers, fully acknowledges the power of this "table," the presence of the Lord in that holy consecration, a dogma formulated over a thousand years ago—the Eucharist. For two thousand years, there has been the Eucharist and a Church celebrating it, and through the Eucharist witnessing Christ to the entire world.

Sitting beside my children in the dimly lit megachurch balcony, looking down at the table, I reflected again and again upon how our two churches hold different beliefs concerning the Eucharist. As I have come to experience these two manifestations of Christianity, I realize how close in intent we really are. In my experience of the Evangelical world, I have often found only slight theological differences, certainly much smaller than many on either side are willing to admit. We both believe in what Jesus' sacrifice represented in terms of our salvation, we both agree that Jesus instituted something special at a Last Supper that he intended to be repeated, and we honor our Lord by using his very own words in our remembrance.

Why, then, do Evangelicals follow those who at the time of the Reformation rejected Catholic doctrine on the Eucharist?

I suggest two reasons, one historical, the other theological.

Many still live with tensions dating back to the Reformation. A legitimate protest against abuses in the Church such as the selling of indulgences spiraled into mutual condemnation and excommunication, leaving many within the infant "reformed" congregations unable to receive the very body and blood of Christ in the Eucharist. Even though reforms instituted by the Council of Trent addressed many of the Reformers' criticisms, the attempts on both sides to reconcile fell on ears that no longer listened to each other. If we consider the impact that must have befallen one-time Catholics now cut off from the sacrament, it is no wonder that the meaning, power, and importance of the Eucharist had to be diminished.

That said, in 1999, hundreds of years after the initial divide, the Catholic Church and the Lutheran World Federation reached an agreement, published as the *Joint Declaration on the Doctrine of Justification*, that ended the mutual anathemas. Subsequently, several other Protestant churches have also subscribed to the Declaration.

Oh how, for my children's sake, for my new Evangelical congregation's sake, I wish that agreement could reach its fulfillment within the Christian family today. What if we could get past our anger and mistrust and appreciate our common Christian background? What if we could acknowledge who we truly are today, not as we think we are based upon errors—on both sides—from the past? And if that reconsideration leads my Evangelical brothers and sisters toward the fullness of at least this one sacrament, what joy there would be in my heart, and (I believe) in heaven.

Theologically, during my decade-long experience in two Evangelical churches, denial of Jesus' "real presence" in the Eucharist has haunted me. What doctrinal issues trouble Evangelicals? Before attending an Evangelical church, I had only half-understandings and poor assumptions to guide me. But I now realize there are two issues at hand. The first issue resembles the reservation some Protestants have about the Catholic custom of displaying lifelike representations of Jesus' body upon the crucifix. Many consider such graphic images to touch upon idolatry, as does believing that the Eucharist is worthy of worship because, they believe, it is only a wafer and cup of wine. This is, of course, a valid concern—if anyone indeed did worship a piece of bread and a chalice of wine.

But, we do not. We worship the Body and Blood of our Lord, of God the Son. It is not idolatry to worship God. It is a responsibility.

In my newfound avenues of biblical study, among other statements commenting on the Real Presence, we have the following from St. Paul:

> Therefore, my dear friends, flee from the worship of idols. I speak as to sensible people; judge for yourselves what I say. The cup of blessing that we bless, is it not a sharing in the blood of Christ? The bread that we break, is it not a sharing in the body of Christ? (1 Cor 10:14-16)

The host and chalice are not idols that Catholics worship. People who drink from the "cup of blessing" and break the Eucharistic bread, Paul says, are "sensible." It is "a sharing in the body of Christ." Christ is not an idol.

The second issue follows from how one understands idolatry. If we do accept that the Eucharist is not merely symbolic but the very body of Christ, then the priest's role takes on a heightened significance. Catholic clergy, connected with the apostles via an unbroken chain of succession, validly perform the consecration of the bread and wine. Evangelical pastors sidestep this issue in their communion ritual, which they consider to be a reenactment of the Lord's Table, not a continuation of Christ's sacrifice on the cross. Therefore, the importance placed upon the Eucharist is reflected in the importance of the priest and the Church the priest represents. Those who, for one reason or another, wanted to break from that Church were motivated, of course, to develop a specific view concerning the Eucharist.

Why?

There is another issue, however, that affects not just Christian harmony but how we present the faith to an unbelieving world.

Is it logical to believe in the Real Presence?

In a world focused more on the spiritual than the physical, upon feelings rather than on sensate realities, can we and should we accept the physical nature of the

Eucharist? Why would God present himself through physical material like bread and wine?

Some question the Real Presence by citing John 6:63: "It is the spirit that gives life; the flesh is useless." They interpret this verse to mean that God does not need to use the physical world for his spiritual purposes. Such an interpretation, however, ignores that fact that God indeed has done so. God the Son did enter the world as a *physical* person, Jesus of Nazareth. He did this to demonstrate his love for us, we who are *physical* creatures ourselves. So, then, it is not strange to consider that God (the Son) so loves us in the world today that he continues to provide himself through the physical Eucharist. This sacrament, by re-presenting his one sacrifice on the cross, fortifies us with heavenly physical food. The Eucharist also provides a special way for him to remain with me, with each of us. By it he can be with us and we can be with him, a physical human being like us.

I used to understand receiving the Eucharist as *my* going and *my* receiving. If I left the altar feeling no different, not feeling Christ's strength, if the Eucharist didn't seem to do me any good at that moment, I questioned whether the Eucharist is real. I now realize, however, that the Eucharist is *God's* way of *coming* to us, of *meeting* us, of *reaching* out and *touching* us. How fitting that an eternal God, having once lived and enjoyed a physical life with human family and friends during his time on earth, created a way to be present physically with his new beloved family and friends in each generation.

Imagine a father with a beautiful child. Imagine his joy at hugging and kissing that infant, the soft touch of the baby's hands. But the parent is called away on a lengthy assignment. He can see the child's picture, maybe visit via video or talk over the phone. But for an agonizing period he is denied the child's touch. He can communicate, give the child all that is needed financially, remain every bit the child's father. But he would still long for that *touch*. That, I believe, is why Christ preserved a way to touch each of us physically down through the ages. We really are his friends and loved ones and children, just as Joseph and Mary, John and James, Peter and Andrew were. Could he would want our relationship with him to be any less than he had with them?

In receiving the Body and Blood in the Eucharist, we are saying to our best friend, our brother, "Yes, I accept your request for a hug, a kiss on the cheek, and a hearty slap on the back." Jesus sees us, right now, in the same way he saw his mother and father, and his first apostles. As he shared family and friendship with them, spiritually (for us now through the Holy Spirit), and through dialog and conversation (for us now through the Bible and our prayer life), he also shared himself physically with them and now also *begs* us for this same level of interaction through Holy Communion. We are given the same glorious opportunity that Mary and Joseph welcomed at the manger in Bethlehem, that John and the apostles welcomed at the Last Supper: to embrace Jesus, to touch him, to lay our heads upon his chest, to share the bread and wine of a meal with our very God and Savior.

So, when we might ask ourselves, "What about those times I don't feel a benefit of receiving the Eucharist?"

We should then understand: It is not about me. It is about Jesus. It is *he* who wants a physical relationship with *me*, just as he had with his parents and with his apostles. It is *he* who welcomes us at each Mass with arms opened wide, seeking for his friends.

Can we, as Christians, deny him? Can we, as his friends, say 'no thanks'?

My thinking about the Eucharist was clarified by the Danish theologian Søren Kierkegaard (1813-1855), a member of the post-Reformation Protestant church "establishment." He was passionate about re-stoking the cooling embers of European Christianity. All around him, he saw the triumph of a social Christianity, but little in terms of personal, life-changing Christian faith.

His *A Practice in Christianity* emphasizes that, despite living in a nominally Christian country and continent, his contemporaries did not live Christian lives because they considered Jesus only as a historical figure. He saw Protestants living not with their own personal savior but with a savior eighteen hundred years removed. He argued persuasively that Jesus is not only savior and Lord of our past but is with us today and should be in vital and intimate relationship with our present lives. He believed that Christianity would change our attitudes and behaviors best by living in a state of "contemporarialism" with Jesus.

In other words, we should no longer see Jesus merely as a historical figure, but as a divine person "with us" just as vitally today (a "contemporary") as he was with the apostles. To see ourselves as living contemporarily with Jesus, and he with us; to know Jesus is suffering for us upon that cross *today* and eternally, just as he did that first Good Friday. To know that *this very morning* Christ has risen to power and glory for us as he did that first Easter day.

Kirkegaard's thought explains how it is mistaken to accuse Catholics of not believing that the first "bloody" sacrifice on Calvary was sufficient for our salvation. Catholics simply stress that the sacrifice of an eternal and ever-present Christ never ends. It goes on even to this day and forevermore, for the forgiveness of each generation's sins. Realizing that at this very moment our Lord is hanging on the cross, suffering, dying to save us from our own faults, soon to rise from the dead—how that knowledge would immobilize us in shame and in awe, and change our lives as nothing else could! Realizing that Jesus wants to rise and come to each of *us* physically, as he did with this apostles on Easter, brings the light of that blessed day into each of our days today.

Sacraments

In its section on "The Seven Sacraments of the Church," the *Catechism of the Catholic Church* states:

> Christ instituted the sacraments of the new law.... The seven sacraments touch all the stages and all the important moments of Christian life: they give birth and increase, healing and mission to the Christian's life of faith. (1210)

> The purpose of the sacraments is to sanctify men, to build up the Body of Christ and, finally, to give worship to God (1123).

Just as daily Bible study and weekly services are key components of Evangelical life—practices Catholics should emulate—the key components of Catholic life, the sacraments, have much to offer Evangelicals. Evangelicals consider baptism and some version of "The Lord's Table" to be sacraments, but not the others that Catholics practice. They limit the number of sacraments for two reasons. First, many Evangelicals claim that Catholics fall into the trap of seeking salvation through the rote performance of these sacraments—"doing works"—instead of developing a one-on-one personal relationship with Jesus and the Father.

Second, Evangelicals have a deep suspicion of the hierarchical church, whose clergy are responsible for administering sacraments and have the authority to bar the laity from receiving them. Because they can limit access to the sacraments, some believe the clergy can control an individual believer's access to salvation. Without clergy there would be no sacramental life, and sacraments would have no power, no "efficacy." Because the first Protestant Reformers fought the church hierarchy and clergy, Evangelicals are understandably cautious about accepting Catholic sacramental doctrines.

Dialogue and mutual understanding can happen if Catholics understand this basis for Evangelicals' resistance to the sacraments. Catholics can respect their fellow Christians who want to emphasize their personal relationship with Christ and so reject the idea that anyone—even a priest—might stand between them and the Lord. For example, an Evangelical would ask, if we can go directly to the Lord and ask forgiveness for our sins, why do we need a priest and a sacrament for reconciliation?

Evangelicals can reach out to Catholics by coming to understand the background of the sacraments and the theology that supports them. For example, Catholics don't believe that the priest who presides over a sacrament can block an individual's relationship with God, nor that the physical elements of the sacraments themselves have magical power. The *Catechism* states: "They [the sacraments] are efficacious because in them Christ himself is at work: it is he who baptizes, he who acts in his sacraments in order to communicate the grace that each sacrament signifies" (1127).

Mutual respect and understanding can develop if Evangelicals accept that Catholics see the sacraments not as obstacles between individual believers and God but as channels of their relationship with the Lord. Catholics believe faith and faithfulness (living out our faith) are situations of "and," not "or." They realize God gave a personal call from the Lord *and* the Lord gave other visible avenues and relationships within his Body to support that call.

For example, by considering married life as not merely a human institution but holy and sacramental, the Church provides a way for spouses to maintain their faith in each other and in God even when their relationships are threatened. In the case of reconciliation for sin, the Church recognizes people can accept and internalize forgiveness more effectively if guided to it by another person (the priest) speaking on God's behalf.

These two sacraments also have a basis in scripture. In John's Gospel, Jesus tells the apostles, "If you forgive the sins of any, they are forgiven them; if you retain the sins of any, they are retained" (Jn 20:23). Answering the Pharisees' query about divorce, Jesus said: "Have you not read that the one who made them at the beginning 'made them male and female ... For this reason a man shall leave his father and mother and be joined to his wife, and the two shall become one flesh?' So, they are no longer two, but one flesh. Therefore, what God has joined together, let no one separate" (Mt 19: 4-6). These practices, therefore, have been part of church tradition since the beginning. Jesus himself provided a basis for the sacraments through his own words and through his Church, guided by the Holy Spirit he promised to the apostles.

The sacraments also express basic Christian faith. Christians believe in a Trinity, a God in three Persons— the Father, the Son and the Holy Spirit. And there are three sacraments to acknowledge our union with each of these Persons: the Father, through baptism into his family; the (once physical) Son, through his physical presence in the Eucharist; and the Spirit, through our spiritual union in confirmation.

Catholics also have sacraments of healing, one of Jesus' most critical tasks on earth and a responsibility he passed on to his disciples, once sending them two-by-two into the villages to heal the sick and cast out demons. The Church also provides healing of the sick, which some call the "last rites" or "extreme unction," to heal physical ailments but even more, at life's end, to assure forgiveness for sins and return to communion with God as a person prepares to enter the Church eternal in heaven. Christ provided for reconciliation to enable a person, time and again, to receive spiritual healing for our all-too-human failings and so reenter a state of saving grace with God and union with our earthly Christian family.

Finally, there are two sacraments of mission—one helps a man and woman establish and maintain their life together, and one consecrates and sustains priests and bishops to serve the Lord and the Christian community.

Initiation:	Baptism (Father)
	Eucharist (Son)
	Confirmation (Holy Spirit)
Healing:	Reconciliation (healing of the soul)
	Anointing of the Sick (healing of the body)
Mission:	Marriage
	Holy Orders

Reconciliation

Those born after Vatican II never experienced church life as it used to be, but after the Council life clearly changed for lay Catholics. Change is essential, but one negative consequence of Vatican II has to do with the sacrament of reconciliation. For my generation it has become a "lost art." This beautiful and powerful manifestation of our Christian faith is often ignored.

The sacrament of reconciliation heals. After we, as
Paul said, "make shipwreck of our faith" (1 Tim 1:19), it
restores our souls. The sacrament heals our relationship
with God; and it heals relationships with the Christian
family, the Church. Even more, it allows ourselves to
heal. Of course, people with medically based mental or
emotional maladies need medical treatment. Others who
suffer from trauma or other devastating experiences need
psychiatric help. But many seek the help of counselors
and therapists and psychiatrists (or daytime TV shows)
because they feel guilt, anxiety, and inadequacy.

Most schools of psychological thought focus upon
relieving guilt. Therapists suggest searching our past to
discover the cause of our feelings, the event that triggered
our bad habits, the inadequacy we are trying to overcome,
the anxiety are we trying to hide or ignore or suppress
to protect ourselves. The underlying assumption is that
none of our problems can be our own fault, that had we
been raised in an environment where bad things didn't
happen, we never would have failed or sinned.

Despite the everyday proof we find in ourselves
and in our fellow human beings, it is assumed we can be
selfless, can have perfect tempers, would never shade the
truth for our own advantage. But even as mental health
professionals suggest these comforting but misguided
ideas, our God-given minds don't accept them. We may
leave a therapy session emotionally cleansed (or perhaps
exhausted and numb), but before long the guilt and
anxiety return, for we know at least some tiny part of
our current condition is our own fault. And even if the
whole world was our oyster, we too might end up like a
spoiled billionaire who steals what little his friends pos-

sess, cursing the poor old lady slowly crossing the street for making us ten seconds late to pick up our next coffee, or figuring how to cheat on our spouse.

Therapists advise coming to terms with guilt by accepting ourselves, by forgiving ourselves. But then, late at night, our minds swimming in the dark and finally quiet enough to be honest, we admit we are not very acceptable and our self-forgiveness means nothing. We know that we will sin again and our efforts at improvement will fail because as self-forgiven as we might be, we lack the inner strength for true and lasting improvement.

The final nail in our coffin of self-delusion is knowing instinctively that our primary sin is not against ourselves. What we do might harm us, but in fact we have sinned against and hurt others; we have sinned against and hurt our God. We are told to forgive ourselves but know we need others' forgiveness, and more importantly we need God's forgiveness. Our greatest sin is not that we've made ourselves feel guilty; the sin itself makes us feel guilty. We do not need self-forgiveness that lasts, at best, until the next fifty-minute session. We need eternal forgiveness, available only through Christ.

Contrast efforts at self-healing with the power of the confessional. There we are reminded of the facts that haunt us. We are held accountable for our own failings and called to sincere sorrow for our sins. We are reminded that God loves us and the Lord has paid the price for our true forgiveness, for even the most heinous of crimes. The one party who matters offers forgiveness—God, who truly has the power to forgive those who have sinned against him and his other children.

Eastern philosophies advise reaching inner peace by ignoring the world and looking inside. But if we are honest, we admit that the last place we would ever want to reside is within our prideful, angry, selfish selves—that, as soon as our deep cleansing breaths, yoga stretches, and rhythmic humming have ended, we will be cast back into the unsettled world of our own mind. We can mask our guilt under a cloud of ignorance and deny reality, but to make lasting change and find peace and health, only the forgiveness and strength God can provide will make a lasting and truly positive difference in our natures.

I drive a lot for my job, and I listen way too much to mindless radio. But from time to time I do turn off the noise. When I do, I either fall into prayer, or I don't. And when I don't, well, all I have then are my own thoughts to keep me company and I quickly grow frustrated. My anxiety intensifies, my impatience spreads. But instead, when I stay within the "mind" of God in prayer, I can relax, ask for his support, and edge closer to a sense of real peace.

Christians learn to quell their pride and anger and selfishness by looking not at themselves but toward Christ, before whom pride cannot stand. In the light of God and life within him, the concerns of this world melt away, anger and selfishness burn to nothingness. We can admit to weaknesses and sin because, unlike the inner selves that constantly condemn us, we have found a more powerful Self who will love and forgive us. By admitting our guilt and helplessness, we can swallow our pride and hand over to God our faults. He can then deal with our failings and shape us into creatures more like himself.

C.S. Lewis offers a powerful metaphor for the sacrament of reconciliation. Using an example from World War II, during which he presented radio talks that turned into his classic book, *Mere Christianity*, he described the journey through life as a great naval convoy. The convoy's success or failure requires three things. First, an admiral who knows how to direct the convoy, for the ships will do more good arriving in England with their vital supplies than making port in Tierra del Fuego. Second, each ship needs to follow the convoy rules—obeying the signalmen, for example, to maintain proper distance and speed. Finally, each ship must maintain itself in proper order. Without sufficient fuel, working propellers, a sturdy rudder and the rest, a ship cannot perform properly and will endanger itself and the rest of the convoy.

That analogy illustrates reconciliation. First, we must face the need to consider our own personal "ship" honestly and admit those faults to be repented of and overcome. After receiving this sacrament, the submission and moral growth that accompany our acts of penance help keep our personal ships in working order. The priest, our spiritual adviser, guides our interaction with nearby vessels. He does not simply want us to feel better and to cope with ourselves more effectively. He wants us to maintain ourselves within the human family God designed. His equal concern for the rest of the flock (the "convoy") enables him to guide us in harmony with others to benefit the Church and the world. Because God wants us to reach our intended port by following the plan that the admiral has laid out and so join him for eternity, the Church calls us back when personal sins and interpersonal failures drive us off course. The Church reassures us of God's providence of more than enough fuel for our journey and protects us as we follow God's course across dangerous seas.

Although Evangelicals do not accept reconciliation as a sacrament, I have come to realize that they and Catholics share the same goal, the same fundamental beliefs. Regarding forgiveness and justification, each emphasizes a different aspect of relationship. Evangelicals focus upon personal relationship, of not needing another, like a priest, to be reconciled with God. They understand deeply that each person needs to realize his or her personal sin, to acknowledge the injury sin has caused and take responsibility for their actions to make permanent, deep improvements in their lives and their behaviors.

The Catholic perspective on reconciliation is biblical. In the Old Testament, God wanted his people to be individually holy and wanted to establish personal relationships with them, as reflected in the many stories of heroes of the faith. But scripture also contains detailed descriptions of the role and position of the priesthood and the customs for the community. It specified how the priests, as God's delegates and as representatives of the people, should perform propitiatory sacrifices that would bring the community forgiveness. In this way the Chosen People were assured they were not a collection of persons acting and feeling alone, but one people, one body, called to repentance.

In the New Testament, something similar happens. A new priesthood is instituted, but under a new High Priest who sacrifices himself to reconcile all people to the Father. Lord Jesus, God the Son, came to earth as a human being to establish relationships with each and every person. And his priesthood did not end with him. He commissioned the apostles and those who followed them to carry on his priestly functions in the Church.

The Church provides a bridge between heaven and earth, as well as the social envelope and glue of everyday life. When believers sin, their sins weaken their relationship with God, but also the entire social fabric. It was the genius of Jesus, in part, to invent a way—what we now call the sacrament of reconciliation—whereby particular members could represent the community as agents of healing for the personal and social wounds caused by sin. It is not the priest who forgives. As the *Catechism* states, "Only God forgives sins. Since he is the Son of God, Jesus says of himself, 'The Son of man has authority on earth to forgive sins' and exercises this divine power: 'Your sins are forgiven.' Further, by virtue of his divine authority, he gives this power to men to exercise in his name" (1441).

Luke recounts a moment at the house of Simon the Pharisee when a woman washes Jesus' feet with her tears and dries them with her hair. Simon is scandalized, but Jesus tells him, "I tell you, her sins, which were many, have been forgiven; hence she has shown great love. But the one to whom little is forgiven, loves little." Then he turns to the woman and tells her, "Your sins are forgiven." The shocked guests say, "Who is this who even forgives sins?" (Lk 7: 47-8). Jesus claiming the power to forgive sin led the authorities to put him to death for blasphemy.

And yet Jesus sent out his disciples to carry on and even expand his ministry: healing the sick and proclaiming the good news. He sent his apostles to bring sinners back into God's grace—the primary task and claim of the good news of salvation. The Gospel of Matthew clearly states this role of spiritual healing. Singling out Peter, Jesus tells the apostles, "I will give you the keys of the kingdom of heaven, and whatever you bind on earth will be bound in heaven, and whatever you loose on earth will be loosed in heaven" (Mt: 16:19). After the resurrection, Jesus reiterates this commission in John 20:21-23, this time for all his apostles, "Again Jesus said, 'Peace be with you! As the Father has sent me, I am sending you.' And with that he breathed on them and said, 'Receive the Holy Spirit. If you forgive anyone's sins, their sins are forgiven; if you do not forgive them, they are not forgiven'."

Paul also describes the role of the church leadership concerning reconciliation:

> All this is from God, who reconciled us to himself through Christ, and has given us the ministry of reconciliation; that is, in Christ God was reconciling the world to himself, not counting their trespasses against them, and entrusting the message of reconciliation to us. So we are ambassadors for Christ, since God is making his appeal through us; we entreat you on behalf of Christ, be reconciled to God. For our sake he made him to be sin who knew no sin, so that in him we might become the righteousness of God. (2 Cor 5:18-21)

As a father who has had to divide time between two faith families, and having experienced first-hand the benefits of sacramental reconciliation, I want to share with my children the reality of sin and forgiveness. As C.S. Lewis noted in *The Screwtape Letters*, "It does not matter how small the sins are provided that their cumulative effect is to edge the man away from the Light and out into the Nothing" (Letter 12). Like dry rot in the timbers of a ship, the damage caused by sin will eventually make the vessel unseaworthy. But Lewis also notes, "By repenting, one acknowledges them as sins—therefore not to be repeated."[13] Reconciliation not only stops the rot but repairs the damage. I want my children to realize that sin is a personal failure before God, but also a failure against the Bride of Christ. Those who ask for God's forgiveness in private may reach eternal bliss, but in the sacrament of reconciliation I have experienced the dramatic reality of forgiveness and unity with the Church and our fellow brothers and sisters as well.

Milestones

Catholic and Evangelical parents bring up their children differently. Children brought up Catholic generally are baptized as infants. From the very beginning they are immersed in sacramental realties—the Eucharist, reconciliation, and confirmation are milestones toward which Catholic parents prepare their children for years. For all its strength, this sacramental focus also presents a danger.

---

13. *A Year with C. S. Lewis: Daily Readings from His Classic Works* (New York: Harper Collins, 2009), 38.

Some speak of Catholics who have been "sacramental-ized but not evangelized," because often education ceases once the sacraments have been received. As adults, some Catholics lack the ongoing growth and understanding needed to support their faith lives over the long-term. For many, once these milestones are reached, practicing the faith becomes a routine and leads to feelings of a spiritually letdown. The training in faith designed for the 8th or 9th or 10th grade mind is insufficient when a believer faces the questions and challenges of adulthood.

However, such milestones do satisfy important psychological realities that sustain us. Such markers provide focus and motivation for study; they provide a public expression of our successes and establish our belonging to a church-family that will support us. They foster a clear sense of identity—as individual Christians, and as members of Christ's body.

Evangelicals might consider the sacraments not as a replacement for Christ, but as a foundation, an infra-structure, for faith. Catholics should realize that their work as Christians and especially as parents does not end when this firm foundation is laid. Just as professional education and healthy exercise are lifelong necessities, so we must seek ongoing training in the faith.

One Faith to Call Them All

From a Catholic perspective, our Evangelical brothers and sisters have much to offer concerning respect for and study of the scriptures. Catholics have much to learn from their active focus upon spreading their faith—

visibly and with a sense of urgency—to the world. From an Evangelical perspective, I remind them of how Jesus himself taught the good news, established a Church, and for the past two thousand years has ministered to that Church through the Spirit and the sacraments, making life with him not just a mental construct, but a physical reality. The summation of both—word and sacrament— is demonstrated in the story of the two disciples who once met a stranger on the road to Emmaus.

As they walked, the man taught the depressed travelers about the Jesus who had just been crucified, explaining the scriptural prophecies concerning him. But the stranger did not stop there. Following their time of fellowship and instruction, he joined them at the table and blessed and broke the bread and shared it with the two.

With this action "their eyes were opened, and they recognized him.... They said to each other, 'Were not our hearts burning within us while he was talking to us on the road, while he was opening the scriptures to us?'" (Luke 24:31-32).

Realizing that they had met Jesus, their Lord, they rushed back to Jerusalem. "Then they told what had happened on the road, and how *he had been made known to them in the breaking of the bread*" (Lk 24: 30-31, 36, emphasis added). The story the disciples recount is the first celebration of the Eucharist, on the very day of Christ's resurrection. At the very moment Jesus gave thanks and blessed the bread, he disappeared from the disciples' sight; because in truth he was still there, still physically with them in the Eucharist.

And at that moment, regarding the biblical instruction they had just received, the disciples asked each other "were not our hearts burning within us?" It was by the sacrament that the scriptures became real. They were so moved they immediately rushed down the dangerous evening road to the rest of the disciples gathered in Jerusalem. Perhaps the events on the road to Emmaus and at the meal that followed demonstrate the virtues of both my family's churches. Jesus the Evangelical "interpreted to them the things about himself in all the scriptures." And Jesus the Catholic celebrated the first Mass: a liturgy of the Word, and a liturgy of the Eucharist, provided by the Savior himself.

Evangelicals and Catholics profess the same faith. The same Lord and Savior. On Easter day the Lord and Savior showed he is available through both the Word and the physical realities of the sacraments. Called by our one shared faith, we need to use what Jesus gave us not as barriers that separate but as bridges to understanding.

Chapter 6

Conclusion

I titled this book *Challenged to Grow* because to have passion for our faith and the God we serve, we need to acknowledge the fundamental nature of our shared Christian reality and grow in it. The Catholic faith is not a new human invention; it has been passed down by the singular Human in history, Jesus Christ of Nazareth. The Bible that Catholics and Evangelicals both read was written, taught, passed down, and finally codified by those in catholic "unity" at the early ecumenical councils of the Church. The sacraments were established by Christ and those who lived with him, those who led the Church that he commanded them to build. The Holy Spirit used the first apostles and their successors down through the generations to articulate the basis of our faith.

Over an extended period, I have experienced the unique blessing to live with many good people in both Catholic and Evangelical churches. I've heard and seen what each church considers points of division, yet I have come to respect both Christian families and recognize all we have in common. This time has been my own challenge to grow, when I have heard questions and challenges in both directions that those who live only within a single expression of the Christian faith may rarely hear.

I hope this book helps my fellow Catholics understand their Evangelical brethren, and vice versa, for we
all serve the same Lord. As baptized Christians, we live
in the same universal church. Our wounds and divisions
can be healed, must be healed, for it is through that process we not only adhere to our Lord's desires (Jn 17:21),
but we can bring the faith to the wider, hungry world
and through our common service.

New City Press

New City Press is one of more than 20 publishing houses sponsored by the Focolare, a movement founded by Chiara Lubich to help bring about the realization of Jesus' prayer: "That all may be one" (John 17:21). In view of that goal, New City Press publishes books and resources that enrich the lives of people and help all to strive toward the unity of the entire human family. We are a member of the Association of Catholic Publishers.

202 Comforter Blvd.
Hyde Park, NY 12538
www.newcitypress.com

Periodicals
Living City Magazine
www.livingcitymagazine.com

Scan to join our mailing list
for discounts and promotions
or go to
www.newcitypress.com
and click on "join our email list."